How do People Learn?

Dr Jake Reynolds (General Editor)
Dr Lynne Caley
Prof. Robin Mason

Jake Reynolds is Director of E-learning at CPI. He focuses on supporting communication, collaboration and learning among professional peer groups, and in applying new models of learning within organisations. He has a DPhil in information engineering from the University of Oxford, which involved the replication of human forms of intelligence in machines. Before joining CPI, Jake led the capacity building and knowledge management programmes of the United Nations World Conservation Monitoring Centre in Cambridge.

Lynne Caley is Director of Professional Development at CPI. Her experience was gained by working in both the health and education sectors. She has a first degree in economics, a masters in education and has completed a doctorate in work-related learning. Lynne's particular interest lies in the transferability of learning from one context to another, particularly with reference to formal and non-formal workplace learning. Lynne has led the development of a number of innovative programmes leading to University awards.

Robin Mason is a Senior Associate of CPI and Professor of Educational Technology at the Open University. She was one of the early pioneers of online teaching and learning, completing one of the very first PhDs on the subject in 1989. Since then she has published prolifically on the Web, in journal articles and in five books. Robin has worked with many teams across the Open University in the design, tutoring and evaluation of online courses. She is currently Director of the Open University's Masters in Open and Distance Education.

Cambridge Programme for Industry (CPI) is the university's provider of continuing professional education to industry and government. Founded in 1988, it is an integral part of the university's lifelong learning provision and pioneers closer links with business, industry and the professions. CPI works with a select group of organisations at the leading edge of their sectors to help them develop their employees against a range of corporate and professional development objectives. It has built up a strong reputation for quality based on its powerful, multi-disciplinary, multi-partner model, informed by applied research.

The Chartered Institute of Personnel and Development is the leading publisher of books and reports for personnel and training professionals, students, and all those concerned with the effective management and development of people at work. For full details of all our titles, please contact the Publishing Department:

Tel: 020 8263 3387
Fax: 020 8263 3850

E-mail: publish@cipd.co.uk

The catalogue of all CIPD titles can be viewed on the CIPD website:
www.cipd.co.uk/bookstore

How do People Learn?

Dr Jake Reynolds (General Editor)

Dr Lynne Caley

Prof. Robin Mason

Cambridge Programme for Industry

First published 2002
Reprinted 2002, 2004, 2007

Cover design by Curve
Designed and typeset by Beacon GDT
Printed in Great Britain by Short Run Press

British Library Cataloguing in Publication Data
A catalogue record for this book is available from the British Library

ISBN 0 85292 956 0
ISBN13 978 0 85292 956 8

Chartered Institute of Personnel and Development,
CIPD House, Camp Road, London SW19 4UX

Tel: 020 8971 9000
Fax: 020 8263 3333
Website: www.cipd.co.uk

Incorporated by Royal Charter. Registered charity no. 1079797.

Contents

Acknowledgements

The authors would particularly like to thank Martyn Sloman of the CIPD for his support and encouragement throughout the production of this report, and for his suggestions on the report's style and focus. They would also like to thank John Kanefsky of the ESRC's Teaching and Learning Research Programme and John Stevens of the CIPD for their contributions during the early drafting stages. Mary James of the University of Cambridge School of Education and Scott Taylor of the Open University Business School also provided extremely helpful reviews of the report, for which the authors are very grateful. Last, a very special thanks to Paul Turner and all those members of the CIPD's Advisory Panel on Learning, Training and Development who gave up their time to review the report and participate in an exciting series of telephone interviews: Ian Canning, Graeme Finnie, Gillian Henchley, Danny Kalman, Neil Offley, Helen Pitcher, David Slingo and Jennifer Taylor.

Foreword

Two significant developments are combining to demand a new approach to the effective delivery of training in organisations. The first is a shifting business model: the way that organisations compete and society advances. The second is a step-change in the capability and potential of technology-based training. Together, these developments are transforming the world of the trainer. All of the 40,000 CIPD members who state that their key responsibilities involve training are well aware that they are living in a time of transition. All will recognise that this is a time of opportunities as well as threats: we must take action to shape the future.

One inevitable consequence will be a shift in focus to the individual learner. He or she will be encouraged and, in many organisations, required to take greater ownership of his or her own learning and development. The training specialist, and other human resource professionals, will be responsible for ensuring that this shift in responsibility can take place. In order to do this effectively we shall need to be far more thoughtful in our approach and gain a fuller understanding of how people do and can learn at work. A renewed awareness of the theoretical background is needed. So too is more effectively focused and relevant research, and an improved transfer of knowledge between research and practitioner.

This report was commissioned to support and encourage this dialogue. Its primary audience is the human resource professional who is seeking to resolve the many practical questions that arise daily in implementing new approaches to learning in organisations. I know, from my own recent experience as a training director in a large organisation, that the pressure can be acute. In

particular, e-learning has been over-sold and over-hyped and its contribution misunderstood. However, the potential is enormous. To quote a member of our expert panel: 'In amongst the noise we are experiencing a new dawn; occasioned by the catalytic effect of e-learning. It is certainly right that we take time to reflect on what we know and ask questions of ourselves.'

Such reflection is essential if we are to resolve the many implementation problems that are emerging in the transition in training and learning. A whole new vocabulary is being created: we need to make sense of it and be prepared to reject those terms that lack substance or add little to our capabilities to do our job. This process will require a return to the theory that underpins our work.

Blended learning offers a good example. It is, at the time of writing, the current buzzword. Problems with learner acceptance of new learning technology have become evident. Therefore, rather than relying on e-learning alone, the solution is to blend it with other more traditional forms of learning – the classroom and on-the-job training. With one bound Jack was free! However, making sense of blended learning is a major task. It is in danger of becoming yet another human resource concept in search of an application. One is reminded of the quip used by former US Labor Secretary Robert Reich: 'Rarely has a term moved from obscurity to meaninglessness without passing through an intervening period of coherence.'[1]

This report can indeed help the training professional make sense of blended learning. It should also assist the profession by bringing a more effective critical faculty to bear and by restoring the balance from technology-led systems

1 Imprecision is not, however, the exclusive property of the trainer, and Robert Reich used the phrase twice in a four-month period – first at the OECD Conference in Paris (June 1994) to describe flexibility, then at the National Alliance of Business in Dallas (September 1994) to describe competitiveness.

to learning and the learner. It does not, however, offer the trainer immediate guidance in the form of checklists and templates; that is not its purpose. What it should do is assist thoughtful professionals to chart their path in their organisation with greater confidence.

A second purpose, as has been stated, is to improve the dialogue between the research community and the practitioner. It is a tragedy that so much of the energy on learning research in universities has so little influence on the practitioner. With some powerful exceptions the two communities seem to work in isolation. This is no longer good enough. A much greater sharing of information and ideas is essential if the research is to be of practical value and practitioner behaviour is to be better informed. We are therefore very pleased that the Teaching and Learning Research Programme (TLRP) of the Economic and Social Research Council will be supporting the CIPD in taking forward the dialogue between the two communities. This will be of considerable mutual benefit, and we are grateful to the TLRP for this commitment.

In short, although this is a research report, we hope that it will be judged in terms of its practical impact. It is intended to raise the level of debate, demystifying a complex topic, and to provide a better platform for considered action in the organisation. Cambridge Programme for Industry (CPI), whom the CIPD commissioned to produce the report, were given a most demanding remit. My thanks to them for the energy and dedication that they have demonstrated throughout the project – from conception to completion.

Martyn Sloman

Adviser, Learning, Training and Development

Executive summary

As many training and development practitioners will attest, learning and training are quite different phenomena. Whereas learning is considered to be the process by which a person constructs new skills, knowledge and capabilities, training is one of a portfolio of responses an organisation can undertake to *promote* learning. But that simple phrase, 'constructs new skills, knowledge and capabilities', hardly does justice to the complex and puzzling process of learning and adaptation that is so much part of our identity as human beings.

Learning is not a mechanical process, nor one that can be described in terms of the shifting of commodities – in this case information – from one person to the next, or between people and computers. This realisation makes the business of training and development more complicated. It suggests the need for a richer understanding of the body of theoretical work that attempts to explain how people adapt their behaviour.

Recognising that the theoretical foundations of learning are not the central focus of the HRD profession, this report brings together key contributions to the field in a single source. As such, it equips training and development practitioners with the theoretical priming they need to chart a course through the large and sometimes conflicting literature that has arisen since learning became the subject of modern enquiry.

In exploring the theoretical foundations of learning, the report aims to take the debate about the future direction of training and development to a higher level. It is intended to challenge the assumptions implicit in conventional practice by drawing attention to theoretical work on the value of alternative (and complementary) approaches to instruction. The report is not exhaustive: it seeks out the contributions that have most to offer to the practitioner, and traces their roots back to early pioneering work.

Naturally, learning theories do not in themselves lead to innovative practice. A number of complexities come into play in any real situation, not least the culture of the organisation, the motivation of its employees and the learning styles and attitudes that they display. This report explores these factors from both theoretical and practical perspectives, but does not attempt to make formal recommendations to organisations.

Few training and development practitioners can fail to have observed, or been affected by, the explosion of interest in learning technologies. While the primary focus of this report remains the nature of learning itself, important questions about cost, quality and effectiveness are raised by the e-learning phenomenon. This report explores some of its benefits and risks, and takes a critical look at the myths that have grown up around it. In examining whether e-learning can be explained in current terms, or whether it requires new theoretical models, the report asks: how different is e-learning?

A brief description of each chapter follows.

Background and context

- An organisation's human capital – the knowledge, skills, competencies, relationships and creativities invested in its people – has emerged as a key competitive factor.

- The task of training and development practitioners is to invest in human capital by facilitating learning in their organisations; yet conventional methods may not be able to achieve this at the required rate.

- Theoretical work, emphasising the experiential and social nature of learning, promises to guide training and development practice through the challenging transformation ahead.

Theories of learning

◪ The major theoretical stances on learning may be structured within four 'clusters' that describe what is common in human learning. The clusters view learning in terms of behaviour, understanding, knowledge construction and social practice, respectively.

◪ The clusters may be analysed in terms of their practical application to learning *for*, *at* and *through* work, allowing well-known training and development techniques to be traced back to their theoretical origins.

◪ The clusters may be analysed also in terms of the key dilemmas that arise during application, including limitations, constraints and contradictions.

Learning in practice

◪ Learning is deeply affected by the context in which it occurs. As well as the specific nature of the learning experience itself, contributing factors include organisational culture, support for learners, employee motivation, and the physical environment.

◪ Motivation is both a determinant and an outcome of achievement. In the right context, and with effective support and reward mechanisms, learning can motivate staff by enhancing their ability to achieve goals.

◪ Learners have characteristic strengths and preferences in the ways they take in and process information – known as learning styles. Learners are not fixed in one style, and will benefit from exposure to a full range of approaches.

How different is e-learning?

◪ Although e-learning builds on over 150 years of practice of distance education, it differs markedly from previous technological innovations and does not yet have an established research base.

◪ So far, e-learning has not produced a new theory of learning; in its present form it can be analysed and interpreted using existing theoretical models.

◪ E-learning has, however, defined a new paradigm for learning; a way of working, studying and problem-solving that reflects the growing connectivity of people and learning resources.

Closing perspectives

◪ As an approach to workplace learning, instruction, by itself, is inadequate to 'deliver' learning in the new competitive environment. Greater experimentation with alternative and richer mixes of learning processes is needed, in particular blends of self-directed, experiential and socially mediated learning.

◪ Informal learning through work, through teams and through other forms of social co-operation has been seriously underestimated. The value of *working* together is well recognised; we now need to recognise the value of *learning* together in physical, virtual or mixed communities.

◪ The idea that e-learning would deliver efficiency gains simply by replacing face-to-face training by technology, has largely been discredited. Its value in providing flexibility is clear, but the new challenge is to capitalise on its support for interactivity.

1 | Background and context

> One must learn by doing the thing; for though you think you know it,
> you have no certainty until you try.
>
> *Sophocles, 496–406 BC (Chorus, Trachiniae)*

◘ **An organisation's human capital – the knowledge, skills, competencies, relationships and creativities invested in its people – has emerged as a key competitive factor.**

◘ **The task of training and development practitioners is to invest in human capital by facilitating learning in their organisations; yet conventional methods may not be able to achieve this at the required rate.**

◘ **Theoretical work, emphasising the experiential and social nature of learning, promises to guide training and development practice through the challenging transformation ahead.**

All human beings have direct experience of learning, sometimes abrupt, following a particular action or event, sometimes gradual, through subtle realisations and moments of awareness. The experience may have been encouraged by external structures and inputs, including formal education and training. It may have been provoked by interaction with other people, or be entirely self-driven. The evidence of learning in individuals is both empirical and anecdotal, and is one of our most distinctive characteristics as a species. It has given rise to a rich, cross-disciplinary literature linking together the disciplines of philosophy, psychology, sociology, education, neuroscience, computer science and management science.

Arguably, organisations also learn, if by no other measure than the combined learning of their employees. To make a corporate asset out of employee learning, however, a web of connections across the organisation is needed (equivalent to the signalling mechanisms of bees in a hive), linked to a culture of transparency and co-operation. The organisation can be said to be learning when the knowledge invested in its people, relationships, culture, systems and visible resources are not only accessible to employees, but are *utilised* by them to support and improve the business. This dynamic area of study has also resulted in a rich and expanding literature.

Interaction, or indeed alignment, between employee and organisational learning has particular importance for training and development practitioners, since it provides the essential inspiration for their work and the context in which it is delivered. Yet few practitioners have the time to research the complex relationship between personal and organisational learning; subject to powerful economic drivers, growing competition for human resources and rapid technological advancement, their organisations need solutions here and now.

Under mounting pressures from within and outside the firm, the need to innovate is being keenly felt by training and development practitioners. Courses are being cut from two weeks to as many hours.

> 'A balance of 'push' and 'pull' approaches
> are evolving to supply employees with
> critical information...'

Technologies are being implemented to personalise learning resources to individual needs. A balance of 'push' and 'pull' approaches are evolving to supply employees with critical information, while enabling them to pursue their own inquiries. Most fundamentally, the boundaries between formal and informal learning are being reviewed, and communities of practice are being heralded as the future engine rooms of learning in some organisations.

It is important to understand why these new approaches have arisen. Why, for example, are courses becoming less fashionable than communities? Where does this leave the conventional model of classroom instruction? What are the opportunities and risks of 'e' or technology-enabled learning? This report reflects the view that to design new approaches to learning – to advance to the next stage of training and development practice – one must first understand the nature of learning itself. Starting from first principles, it is reasonable to expect that effective learning processes can be developed.

Human capital

The view of learning as investment in an organisation's future is captured neatly in the phrase 'human capital', introduced by American economist Theodore W. Schultz in 1961, and elaborated shortly afterwards by Gary S. Becker (1964) (both men went on to become Nobel Laureates). In his pioneering paper, Schultz noted:

Truly, the most distinctive feature of our economic system is the growth of human capital. Without it there would be only hard, manual work and poverty except for those who have income or property. (Schultz 1961: 16.)

Human capital spans the knowledge, skills, competencies, relationships and creativities implicit in an organisation's workforce. Like other forms of capital, it is susceptible to depreciation. The main difference with other forms of capital lies in management. Humans are not assets in the strict sense, to be purchased, exploited and controlled: they are free to act independently within certain boundaries, and free to move on (ICAEW 2001).

Many companies have now come to regard human capital as their greatest competitive asset. In knowledge-based sectors such as software, bioscience and consultancy, it is easy to see why: their key capital *is* human capital. In other sectors such as energy, manufacturing, distribution or banking, the link is less obvious: human capital may be dwarfed by investments in infrastructure, technology and equipment or large-scale financial reserves. However, were the phrase to be replaced by 'ability to recognise and respond creatively to change' (the entrepreneurial instinct), most companies would recognise this as a competitive asset. As Becker noted in a recent interview:

The most successful companies and the most successful countries will be those that manage human capital in the most effective and efficient fashion – investing in their workers, encouraging workers to invest in themselves, provide a good learning environment, and yes, include social capital as well as skills and training. (Becker 2001.)

Box 1: Learning in the connected economy

Many of the changes taking place in companies over the past decade have been attributed to the effects of the 'new', 'global' or 'knowledge' economy, or more recently the 'connected' economy, the driving forces of which are held to be:

- greater access to communications, media and computing power
- fewer barriers to international trade/global markets
- increased speed and agility of organisations
- greater competition, globally
- fuzzier boundaries between suppliers, clients, partners and competitors.

Although the boundary between new and old, global and local, connected and unconnected, remains extremely uneven, some common challenges for learning professionals have arisen:

- equipping employees rapidly with new skills and knowledge
- personalising and contextualising learning experiences
- unlocking individual knowledge for collective benefit
- linking formal and informal learning processes
- supporting learning among a distributed and mobile workforce
- harnessing technologies to add value to learning processes
- enabling employees to take charge of their own learning
- gaining the attention of employees in an increasingly information-rich workplace.

These challenges will be met through a complex web of strategic and tactical decisions leading to the transformation of learning processes in organisations.

Conventionally, attempts to increase human capital result in training programmes designed to boost quality, efficiency or marketing success, to increase technical skills or contribute to professional or managerial development. In the main, programmes are delivered *to* employees in the form of discrete courses, events or literature designed to cover gaps in the organisation's capability.

For a variety of reasons, this model is now proving unsatisfactory for many companies. The competitive landscape in which the companies operate has changed radically in some sectors: it is now characterised by global competition, complex and dynamic markets, rapid technological innovation, distributed workforces and rising stakeholder expectations. In conditions of frequent, often unpredictable change, learning is neither a luxury nor a secondary issue – it is one of the axes on which the future of the company will be decided. As business writer Charles Leadbeater recently put it:

Companies increasingly rest on their ability to excite and combine the intelligence and ideas of the people who work for them, to devise new products and services. (Leadbeater 2001.)

The association between learning and change is fundamental to the current restructuring of learning within organisations. As operating environments change, skills need to be updated and knowledge renewed on increasingly short cycles. The shelf-life of some knowledge can be measured in months or weeks; in the case of some financial information, it might be measured in minutes. The requirement to replenish knowledge rapidly and continuously is a major challenge. The fact that conventional training and development methods – in particular those based upon

'As a vehicle for creating and sustaining human capital, self-directed learning is clearly very important.'

instruction – may be unable to achieve this is cause for concern, and one of the reasons why alternative approaches are becoming popular.

One of the most interesting departures from conventional practice is the movement towards greater *self-direction* in learning (see Chapter 3). Three realisations are driving this debate:

1 learning is more or less continuous and anchored in work

2 the person best able to define and act upon their learning requirements is the learner him- or herself

3 self-driven achievement is a powerful, if not the most powerful, motivator of learning.

As a vehicle for creating and sustaining human capital, self-directed learning is clearly very important. Yet it is much easier to envisage than to implement. The remainder of this chapter explores the nature of knowledge and learning in order to understand what new approaches might accelerate the movement to self-directed learning.

Dimensions of learning
What is knowledge?

The concept of knowledge has many facets and dimensions. It is bound up with the context in which it is gained and the use to which it is put. For the purposes of this report, knowledge may be defined as the *product of a learning experience*. It may not be the sole product: skills, capability, performance, trust and relationships may also result. Language which expresses knowledge as an abstracted form of information (itself an abstracted form of data) is problematic since it suggests that knowledge is a transferable

commodity. Mere exposure to a book or other learning resource does not guarantee learning, nor any increase in knowledge. Many would argue that knowledge – as a human trait – cannot exist outside the human brain.

By forming a distinction between *knowing that* and *knowing how*, Oxford philosopher Gilbert Ryle's seminal study of 1949 throws light on this discussion. Ryle's belief that the two forms of knowledge were separate but equal put him at odds with the almost universal acceptance at the time of the superiority of intellectual rather than practical knowledge, the superiority of *that* over *how*. Most educational systems, including those in the United Kingdom, are founded on this intellectualist assumption, and they resonate throughout the current debate about vocational skills and competence:

Learning how or improving in ability is not like learning that or acquiring information. Truths can be imparted, procedures can only be inculcated, and while inculcation is a gradual process, imparting is relatively sudden. It makes sense to ask at what moment someone became apprised of the truth, but not to ask at what moment someone acquired a skill. 'Part-trained' is a significant phrase, 'part-informed' is not. Training is the art of setting tasks which the pupils have not yet accomplished but are not any longer quite incapable of accomplishing. (Ryle 1949: 59.)

Ryle gave the example of learning how to be a surgeon:

A man knowing little or nothing of medical science could not be a good surgeon, but excellence in surgery is not the same thing as knowledge of medical science; nor is it a simple product of it. The surgeon must indeed have learned from instruction, or by his own inductions and observations, a great number of truths; but he must also have learned by practice a great number of aptitudes. (Ryle 1949: 49.)

Ryle's *that* is close to the idea of 'embrained' knowledge identified by British management scientists Frank Blackler (1995) and Alice Lam (2000); in other words explicit facts, observations and propositions absorbed from the public domain through a process of individual cognition. Good examples include scientific knowledge like the theory of electromagnetism, or principles of evolution. Both authors recognise a second form of explicit knowledge described as 'encoded'. This knowledge is located in the organisation's collective rules, procedures, and flows of information. Because it is codified, it represents only a partial picture of the organisation's true functioning, not its full complexity.

It is Ryle's *how* that has eluded definition, in particular his notion of 'practical knowledge'. This knowledge is regarded as tacit, or not amenable to codification. Lam usefully resolves tacit knowledge into two forms: 'embodied' knowledge which is individually generated; and 'embedded' knowledge which is socially constructed, and collectively held. Both forms of tacit knowledge concern the mastery of procedures and systems, such as might be necessary to get a decision made in a complex organisation or to solve a rarely occurring problem. Both forms allow people to understand and adapt to change, to maintain control and to practise skills; the things that make them effective.

Although Ryle's concept of *how* originally concerned the individual, the recognition of collectively held tacit knowledge is an important refinement of his idea. Unwritten cultural norms,

beliefs, traditions and socially constructed know-how are examples of embedded knowledge; not traceable to individuals or to information resources, dynamic and distributed, embedded knowledge is easy to overlook. Figure 1 depicts a simplified version of Lam's typology of knowledge.

The distinction between *knowing how* and *knowing that* is valuable because it helps us to understand what makes learning effective. *Knowing how* is inextricably linked to performance – to competent practice – and therefore cannot be separated from the context in which it arises or is applied. It is the tacit knowledge produced by solving problems of a practical rather than abstract nature, and extends beyond common sense into the mastery of situations.

Learning from novelty

Successful learning tends to happen when an individual reacts to opportunities. The result depends upon the individual's capacity and readiness to learn, and hence upon the task and setting. The more novel the task, the greater the understanding required and the more challenging the range of solutions; thus the greater the learning potential. Experience aids learning by making it possible to recognise and deal with novelty bound up in tasks – in other words to cope with new situations. Equally, it builds familiarity

Figure 1 | Typology of knowledge (adapted from Lam 2000)

	Individual	Collective
Explicit	Embrained	Encoded
Tacit	Embodied	Embedded

into some or more elements of a task, helping to automate them. Over time, a task may become so routine that it no longer requires conscious control. Reading is a good example. Efficient reading occurs when the habitual perceptual operations required for scanning consume little or no mental effort. Only when a word is out of place or a typo appears do we become aware of the complexity of the process.

Many theorists (including Dreyfus and Dreyfus 1986; Dewey 1969; and Schön 1983) maintain that learning involves a progression from novice-to-expert status, from detail to total situation, a sequence culminating in *instinctive action*. Both Dewey and Schön focus on the need to evaluate one's own development by what they call 'implicit monitoring' (Schön 1983). Familiar tasks can then be processed rapidly, freeing up time and mental capacity to deal with novelty:

The practitioner allows himself to experience surprise, puzzlement, or confusion in a situation which he finds uncertain or unique. He reflects on the phenomenon before him, and on the prior understandings which have been implicit in his behaviour. He carries out an experiment which serves to generate both a new understanding of the phenomenon and a change in the situation. (Schön 1983: 68.)

Instinctive action depends on a high degree of tacit knowledge about a task, allowing the individual to navigate complex problems with ease and transfer their understanding from one situation to another. Such is the value of tacit knowledge that organisations have devoted a great deal of attention over the past five years to making it explicit, with mixed results. By sharing personally acquired knowledge with colleagues, Nonaka and Takeuchi (1995) suggest, the Japanese are particularly good at making this conversion.

Learning through experience

Mistakes are a valuable source of learning. They are evidence of practice, of action and experimentation. To make the same mistake twice, however, is considered foolish as it would seem that learning has not taken place. Along with other possible outcomes, then, mistakes create authentic and often very personal experiences for individuals to reflect upon, grow to understand, and draw lessons from for future actions.

Figure 2 | Experiential learning cycle (adapted from Kolb 1984)

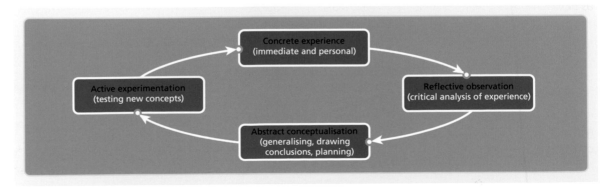

> 'Cultures that take a dim view of failure may not provide the conditions necessary to support natural learning...'

Building on the intellectual foundations of John Dewey, Kurt Lewin and Jean Piaget, the American organisational behaviour specialist, David A. Kolb, brought together an explanation of this process – known as *experiential learning* – in 1984. The core of Kolb's model is illustrated in Figure 2. It comprises a four-stage 'learning cycle'[1] which shows how experience is transformed, via reflection, into concepts that guide future activity, and hence new experiences. Learning is depicted clearly as a process, not an outcome.

The learning cycle has some limitations. For example, based on preferences and intentions, we know that individuals are selective in their use of experiences and information when forming concepts and planning actions, yet the role of decision-making in the model is not clear. The model also lacks a mechanism for self-directed sourcing of new information during critical reflection. But despite its simplicity – some might say oversimplification[2] – Kolb's model has important implications for training and development; in fact for all education. In his own words:

The fact that learning is a continuous process grounded in experience has important educational implications. Put simply, it implies that all learning is relearning. How easy and tempting it is in designing a course to think of the learner's mind as being blank as the paper on which we scratch our outline. Yet this is not the case. Everyone enters every learning situation with more or less articulate ideas about the topic at hand. We are all psychologists, historians and atomic physicists. It is just that some of our theories are more crude and incorrect than others…one's job as an educator is not only to implant new ideas but also to dispose of or modify old ones. (Kolb 1984: 28.)

Experiential models have yielded a wealth of practical strategies for training and development practitioners (see for example Boud *et al.* 1985; Dennison and Kirk 1990; Schank 1997). They have also helped to bridge the divide between research on human learning and experience-based approaches to artificial intelligence. Roger Schank, for example, developed an interest in human learning after observing the difference between how he was 'training' machines and how schoolchildren are taught in the USA. He advocates a 'learning by doing' model which involves doing, reasoning and self-generated explanation – almost identical to Kolb's experience, reflection and conceptualisation stages. Schank opposes the conventional model of instruction, claiming that:

Nothing anyone says (no matter how eloquent the speaker or insightful the words) will do any more than inspire you. You must internalize procedures to do a better job. To do this you must try them out and receive help when you fail. (Schank 1997: 17.)

Schank draws attention to the value of learning from failure, wherein individuals develop the confidence to take risks and determine their own learning agendas. He describes this as 'natural learning' – the process of getting it right through failure and practice. Rather provocatively, Schank suggests that:

Failing in interesting ways should be a goal of training. (Schank 1997: 127.)

Of course, such suggestions do rather depend on the existence of a culture of experimentation in the workplace. Cultures that take a dim view of failure may not provide the conditions necessary to support natural learning, nor indeed innovation at all.

Learning through social interaction

If learning is driven by experience then it must be in part a social process, since interaction between people is a powerful source of new experience. Not only do personal experiences arise directly in the context of co-operative activities, elements of experience may be relayed through the processes of dialogue and storytelling. Moreover, observation of others' behaviour – their successes and failures – provides an important source of indirect experience that may be used to approximate desired behaviours. Canadian psychologist Albert Bandura, who pioneered a theory of observational (or socially mediated) learning, summarised this in the following way:

Except for elementary reflexes, people are not equipped with inborn repertoires of behavior, they must learn them. New response patterns may be acquired either by direct experience or by observation. (Bandura 1977: 16.)

He went on:

Learning would be exceedingly laborious, not to mention hazardous, if people had to rely solely on the effects of their own actions to inform them what to do…Because people can learn from example what to do, at least in approximate form, before performing any behavior, they are spared needless errors. (Bandura 1977: 22.)

Recognition of the positive effect of social interaction on learning can actually be traced back to the Russian cognitive theorist, Lev S. Vygotsky (1962). In the early 1930s, he discovered that children could perform well beyond their mental age when provided with elementary assistance from an adult or older child[3]. The implication of his experiment is that social interaction greatly enhances an individual's ability to learn within the limits set by their developmental stage (in children) and prior understanding, a finding confirmed by the success of co-operative strategies such as team working and apprenticeship.

Many contributions followed Vygotsky's early work, each taking social learning theory down a different, complementary route (Bandura 1977; Argyris and Schön 1978; Senge 1990; Engestrom and Middleton 1996). The strands were brought together recently by Etienne Wenger (1998) in his account of learning as *social participation*. Together with contributions from John Seely Brown and Paul Duguid (1991), these works form much of the basis of our understanding of *communities of practice*.

The view of learning as social participation is important, because few tasks in an organisation are conducted in isolation from other employees, clients or suppliers, and many are conducted in teams. Even apparently solitary tasks such as long-distance driving involve social interaction at key stages – loading and unloading, communications with base, rest and refreshment – during which essential information is shared, plans formed and new knowledge generated. The swapping of stories in roadside refreshment areas is an effective way of discovering the location of new routes and hazards along the way, and of dealing with isolation. Without support from base and feedback from other drivers, long-distance driving would be stressful and inefficient.

Social interaction is *not* a pre-requisite for all types of learning since there are many sources of experience open to an individual, not all of them socially mediated. Similarly, reflective processes, conceptualisation and experimentation may be conducted independently of other people, as demonstrated by the stereotypical lone researcher, or the child quietly investigating a box of toys. There is no doubt, however, that whether experience is generated directly, through observation, through dialogue or through self-discovery, social interaction is a major amplifier and solidifier of learning.

Learning and training

If learning from experience and learning through social interaction are critical ingredients of learning *what*, then how does this affect training? The terms 'learning' and 'training' clearly have different meanings. Focusing on the individual, learning is the process by which a person constructs new knowledge, skills and capabilities, whereas training is one of several responses an organisation can undertake to *promote* learning. Training and development practitioners may wish to reflect on the degree to which conventional training methods, such as classroom instruction, emphasise experiential learning and social interaction among participants; similarly, on the value they attribute to these methods personally. Moreover, do the conventional methods encourage *self-directed learning*, or is there a danger of setting up a dependency relationship with the training provider?

New approaches to learning
Overview

Instruction lies at the heart of literally thousands of products and services from training and education providers worldwide, many of them very different in scope, emphasis, duration and medium. The archetypal classroom-centred course, itself subject to many variations, is still extremely popular in schools, universities and corporate training centres. At its best it can be a fulfilling environment for

participants to obtain inspiration and new knowledge, and to share experiences and build relationships with peers. But it can also be a very negative experience. Courses that entail near continuous *transmission* of information to participants tend to confine interesting dialogues and story-swapping to refreshment breaks. Similarly, courses that feature large and comprehensive curricula may daunt, overload, and in some cases bore recipients due to a lack of alignment with their personal requirements. Limiting opportunities for resolution of enquiries can also detract from the learning experience, and failure to make arrangements for post-course follow-up and debate tends to isolate training from work.

It is important to recognise that the course itself is not under threat. At its most basic, a course is simply a space of time – not necessarily continuous – in which learners can involve themselves in study. An extremely wide range of learning processes may be employed within the course, only one of which is instruction.

Problems with instruction

The conventional idea of instruction, as exemplified by the 'tell and listen' classroom lecture, dates back to the medieval period when books were in short supply and learned men were given the task of reading extracts to their students. While nothing has replaced it yet, especially in terms of cost-efficiency, the model does suffer from some fundamental deficiencies:

◘ Information flows largely in one direction: insufficient attention is given to the contributions of participants or the formation of constructive dialogues.

- The experience can be largely theoretical: few opportunities exist for action and experimentation.

- Topics may be disconnected from actual challenges and tasks, even when described as work-related.

- Opportunities for social interaction are limited: relationships with peers are established, but not cultivated.

- Courses can be blunt and unwieldy, often too large, too late, and of varying relevance to participants.

- Learning is a continuous process, whereas instruction is discrete.

- There is a tendency for instruction to react to gaps in capability, rather than encourage self-development.

- Instruction can foster a dependency relationship in which the learner waits for instruction rather than takes charge of their own learning agenda. Effectively, this presents a barrier to self-directed learning.

The following sections describe a variety of approaches to workplace learning that are suited to the self-directed learner, and where innovation is particularly noticeable.

Performance support

Some have pronounced the death of the course, or at least its gradual displacement in favour of short, personalised, contextualised, performance-enhancing modules accessed electronically in any place, at any time (Jennings 1999). A number of leading training providers have accepted the inevitability of this transformation and have begun to reshape, resize and repurpose their course materials. This transformation will bring many conveniences to the busy professional learner, such as just-in-time instruction delivered to the desktop or portable device. But while it has significant potential to make instruction more relevant and efficient, electronic performance support does not accommodate the experiential and social dimensions of learning in its present form.

Performance-support models are not intended to foster deep learning and reflection: their main objective is to offer fast and targeted assistance to individuals suffering from a glut of information and a shortage of time. They are, as the name implies, extensions of a person's intellectual machinery, not instruments to transform behaviour. As such, they have the potential to be an immensely valuable resource for self-directed learning, if not a source of learning in their own right.

Experiential approaches

Experiential approaches to learning emphasise reflection on experience, conceptualisation and practice. They stress the benefit of learning by doing, of learning through mistakes, and of observing and emulating others in close proximity. Although classrooms and courses can simulate all the stages of experiential learning, the only authentic source is work itself. Yet the idea of managing experiential learning in the workplace is extremely challenging, and few organisations have invested fully in this approach. Several promising approaches have emerged, however, amongst them: *action learning, performance simulation* and *problem-based learning*.

Action learning

In this approach, pioneered in British coal mines after World War II by Reg Revans, small groups of colleagues formulate approaches to real problems they are encountering in work. They share their experiences of the problem and seek constructive criticism and advice, before putting that advice into practice. The group remains together while the results of the action taken are reviewed, and lessons drawn. Known as a 'set', the group focuses on actual problems of central concern to the organisation and exploits fully the opportunity of social learning within the group. Based on the experience and creativity of the set members, action learning searches for solutions to problems of the 'here and now' rather than case-based approaches – real or simulated – which analyse examples from a different place and time. Set members are conditioned to identify and source the information they need to solve problems as a group, rather than depend on external provision.

Action learning has evolved in many different directions over its 50-year history, yet it retains a set of distinctive principles, even a certain philosophy, as described by Yuri Boshyk (2000):

As a philosophy, business driven action learning is based on the belief and practice that learning should be tied to business realities, and that some of the best business solutions can and should come from fellow executives and employees. Many of the companies that utilise business driven action learning are those who also have a high respect for their people and who appreciate that learning often comes from the sharing of experiences in an open exchange. (Boshyk 2000: xi.)

Performance simulation

This well-established route to experiential learning essentially comes in two forms: electronic simulation, best known for its use in training pilots but now being applied to generic business areas such as strategy, marketing and sales; and role play, which has virtually unlimited application, from medical diagnosis to leadership development. Both forms work by mimicking actual workplace situations in an environment where failure can be analysed and corrected without impacting on real work. Inevitably, the greater the approximation to real-life conditions the more effective the simulation.

While electronic simulations designed for business training currently could not be described as 'immersive', a combination of factors is slowly increasing the realism of the experience:

1   Use of multimedia to recreate features of the physical working environment.

2   Use of artificial intelligence to predict lifelike sequences of events.

3   Increasing plausibility of the scenarios and storylines portrayed.

Electronic simulation is expensive to produce and the tasks selected for simulation must inevitably appeal to large numbers of potential trainees. Where job functions are defined quite precisely (flying is a good example), and the risks of failure great, simulation can be cost-effective. However, job functions that are more diffused (for example, management positions), or which are dynamic in nature, present a moving target for simulation developers. Other than cost, the main drawback in such situations is the difficulty of capturing

> 'The greatest benefit of simulation is that it creates
> the space for trainees to fail gracefully, and analyse
> why this has occurred.'

sufficient domain, organisation and job-specific context in the simulation to deceive the learner into believing the situation is meaningful. Clearly, as an experiential learning vehicle, work itself takes some beating.

Realism is also the central issue with role play. Here, Schank (1997) draws attention to the need to allocate roles very carefully:

You may have experienced a role-playing scenario in which the facilitator points to one trainee and says, 'You be the CEO' and points to another trainee and says, 'You be his subordinate.' Then these same two people play out the scenario by switching roles. The problem, of course, is that neither person knows how to play a CEO – each is about as credible as Jerry Lewis playing Hamlet. When a simulation calls for a CEO, trainers should go out and recruit an ex-CEO. (Schank 1997: 26.)

The greatest benefit of simulation is that it creates the space for trainees to fail gracefully, and analyse why this has occurred. This feature should not be forgotten in role-play scenarios: because they are live and emotionally charged, the prospect of 'failing in interesting ways' in front of peers may not create the positive environment required for learning. Electronic simulation certainly has the edge in this respect.

Problem-based learning

Ordering the learning experience around problem-based activities rather than subjects or disciplines can help to develop the skills necessary to find solutions to real problems. Although the problems may be artificial or historic, and may relate only loosely to immediate priorities, their solution

provides the opportunity to rehearse responses to real situations, emphasising key processes such as problem definition, scenario planning, sourcing information, dialogue, debate and teamworking. Since the problems are not real, this approach can also create the mental space for learners to experiment with new ideas without fearing repercussions.

Complex situations can be presented in a problem-based activity, requiring learners to appreciate the totality of a situation rather than the set of discrete elements presented to them through conventional training. Although learners may be provided with tools and resources to help them learn, they must make their own decisions about how to manage a situation effectively. The underlying philosophy is one of learner-centeredness: the opportunity to direct the learning experience, to develop an independence of enquiry. As Maggi Savin-Baden of Coventry University puts it:

Problem-based learning is increasingly being seen as a means of educating students to learn with complexity. What I mean here is that problem-based learning helps students to see that learning and life takes place in contexts, contexts that affect the kinds of solutions that are available and possible. (Savin-Baden 2001: 15.)

Interest in problem-based approaches has arisen from a number of directions, notably the movement towards self-directed learning led by, among others, Carl Rogers, Malcolm Knowles and Jack Mezirow (see Chapter 3: The motivation to learn). From these foundations, problem-based learning has emerged into a mainstream curricular model in education and training (see Boud and Feletti 1997 for a more detailed analysis).

Socially mediated approaches

The growing popularity of communities of practice suggests that the concept of learning as social practice is emerging into the mainstream. Cynics might observe that the popularity of communities of practice coincides with the growth of the Internet, concluding that they are a by-product of communication networks. But in this case they must have existed at least since the mass production of the telephone. Others view community learning as a bottom-up response to voids created by flatter management hierarchies. The truth is that living and learning in communities is a human trait that has existed for as long as humans have had language, tools and social systems; it is just that organisations have only recently begun to recognise them. Wenger (1998) sees communities of practice as utterly pervasive:

We all belong to communities of practice. At home, at work, at school, in our hobbies – we belong to several communities of practice at any given time. And the communities of practice to which we belong change over the course of our lives. In fact, communities of practice are everywhere. (Wenger 1998: 6.)

One of the defining characteristics of communities is that they create, hold and distribute knowledge in ways that exceed individual capabilities. The real value of community learning is not the management of explicit knowledge, however: it is their potential to link together individuals with common interests and problems, and enable experiences and ideas to flow. In doing so, the composition and identity of the community evolves, and a reason for belonging emerges. Suddenly, an employee in Sydney can locate – and identify with – a colleague in Rio who has worked on a similar problem. Without travel, expense or even significant time, they can work together on a solution.

Knowledge management

The realisation that knowledge is no longer bounded in space and time creates a challenge for organisations: how do we know what we know? Conventionally, this is not a question that has concerned trainers: their task has been to bring *new* learning to the organisation, not to capitalise on what is already known (Weiner 1990). From an experiential learning standpoint, however, it is exactly this last issue which may be critical to organisations.

As Scarborough, Swan and Preston's survey of British companies found in 1999, interest in 'knowledge management' – the capture, use and reuse of knowledge across traditional boundaries – has gradually displaced the high tide of interest in the 'learning organisation' seen during the early 1990s. There are signs here of a reactive process, as one idea responds to its predecessor despite sharing much in common. Whereas learning organisations have tended to innovate *process*, knowledge organisations have focused on *technology* – often with disappointing results. Second-generation knowledge initiatives are now under way, this time emphasising human relationships over 'data', as Collison and Parcell (2001) neatly capture:

The transfer of knowledge is all about people and relationships rather than projects and resources – hence an environment to support knowledge management needs to respect people as people and provide ways for them to key into relationships with others. (Collison and Parcell 2001: 106.)

Second-generation knowledge initiatives share a remarkable amount in common with notions of the learning organisation. The convergence may soon be complete.

Conclusion

As a means of focusing attention on the importance of learning, the prevailing model of instruction is undeniably effective. The challenge now, however, is to identify a suite of new approaches to learning that integrate the most successful aspects of existing practice with current theoretical knowledge about the nature of learning. This heralds the breakdown of boundaries between work, learning and knowledge management.

Realistically, this is going to involve the development of learning interventions that inspire and motivate learners over extended periods of time, and through an appropriate mix of inputs and outputs, individual and collaborative study, formal and informal processes, and a blend of face-to-face and virtual contact. The signs are that this process has begun, in part spurred by the reflection and reanalysis caused by e-learning technologies, and the increasing pressure on training and development practitioners to obtain results.

Already one trend does appear to be more permanent than most: the shift in emphasis from the provider of training and educational opportunities to the learner. Increasingly, trainers will need to step back from the 'benign provider' model, characterised by centrally inspired, generic course delivery, towards a new role as brokers of knowledge-sharing and facilitators of knowledge creation within learning communities. Implicit in this shift is the move to a richer mix of learning processes – among which courses may have an important role – to achieve more sustainable learning outcomes.

To date, community learning has been characterised as much by failure as success, but there is evidence of a growing maturity born through experimentation (a good example is Collison and Parcell 2001). As a complement to instructional approaches, the benefits are clear: they offer a method of transforming discrete interventions into ongoing learning opportunities, and of broadening input into discussions. As a means of driving business performance, the benefits are even clearer: when an organisation knows what it knows, and knows how to make this knowledge available to its employees, then problem-solving and innovation will follow. But disciplined approaches to knowledge management must accompany community learning projects; appropriate communications and knowledge technologies also play an important, if secondary, role.

As might be expected, not all the sources of advice and solutions in workplace learning identify the same trends, nor subscribe to the same vision of how learning processes are likely to evolve. In conditions of uncertainty, confidence can be gained by re-examining what is known about learning at a theoretical level, in other words by returning to first principles, which is the focus of the next chapter.

Endnotes

1 Kolb (1984: 21) attributes this model to Kurt Lewin.

2 An even simpler model was proposed by Terry Borton (1970) consisting of a 'What? – So what? – Now what?' cycle corresponding, presumably, to Kolb's experience, reflection and conceptualisation/planning stages.

3 Vygotsky's work was banned by the Soviet authorities after his death from tuberculosis in 1934. As a result, much of it remained unpublished until the late 1950s.

2 | Theories of learning

Personally I am always ready to learn, although I do not always like being taught.

Winston Churchill, 1874–1965

◘ **The major theoretical stances on learning may be structured within four 'clusters' that describe what is common in human learning. The clusters view learning in terms of behaviour, understanding, knowledge construction and social practice, respectively.**

◘ **The clusters may be analysed in terms of their practical application to learning *for*, *at* and *through* work, allowing well-known training and development techniques to be traced back to their theoretical origins.**

◘ **The clusters may be analysed also in terms of the key dilemmas that arise during application, including limitations, constraints and contradictions.**

Writers and philosophers have been fascinated with the way that we learn since antiquity, and it would be impossible in the space allotted here to visit all of the views that have had currency. Like most things, ideas about learning are subject to fashion; and their popularity can be traced through the rise and fall of social history. Rather than attempt to give a comprehensive picture, this chapter introduces four clusters of theories that have been influential over the past 50 years. Each cluster can be located in a practical setting, and key dilemmas and decisions around its use can be identified.

Using the four clusters – which view learning as behaviour, understanding, knowledge construction and social practice – it is possible to build up a 4 x 3 matrix incorporating their use *for*, *at* and *through* work:

◘ For work: learning outside the workplace that is intended as preparatory or complementary to the work role ('just in case' learning). Typically conducted at the beginning of a career, it also spans learning activities throughout the working life. More broadly interpreted, learning for work occurs through contact with professional bodies, interest groups and external boards and committees of all kinds.

◘ At work: learning opportunities that are offered by the employer or as a consequence of employment, which require work to be set aside in favour of activities that stimulate or simulate (but do not replicate) work tasks.

◘ Through work: learning that occurs through direct work experience, individually or within teams or other collective groupings.

In the past, much research on adult education, particularly in the West, has focused on the *differences* in learning strategy exhibited by people according to the context in which they learn, and their individual disposition and learning styles. The assumption is that the process by which people learn is individual and personal; an assumption that can create huge practical problems in delivery.

> 'Reinforcement is the key feature of the behavioural
> theories, and a reinforcer is anything that
> strengthens the desired response.'

The previous chapter (Chapter 1: Dimensions of learning) outlined some *common* traits of human learning (in other words, what people share), in particular leaning from novelty, from experience, and through social interaction. This chapter adds structure to the discussion by exploring the theoretical basis of these traits in greater depth, allowing the next chapter (Learning in practice) to concentrate on differences.

Learning as behaviour
Overview

This cluster of theories, drawn from the empirical natural sciences, and associated primarily with the work of B.F. Skinner[1], asserts that changes in behaviour are the result of an individual's responses to events (stimuli) and the consequences that ensue (rewards or punishments). A stimulus will be met with a response which, in turn, produces a consequence such as a verbal statement, hitting a ball, or solving a maths problem. When a particular stimulus–response pattern is reinforced (rewarded), the individual is said to become *conditioned* to respond each time the stimulus occurs. Skinner traces the theory back to pioneering experiments on animal intelligence conducted by his inspiration, Edward L. Thorndike (1911), at the very outset of the twentieth century:

A cat enclosed in a box struggled to escape and eventually moved the latch which opened the door. When repeatedly enclosed in a box, the cat gradually ceased to do those things which had proved ineffective ('errors') and eventually made the successful response very quickly. (Skinner 2001.)

Behavioural explanations of learning underpin all other explanations of learning in this chapter. The additional clusters of theory have arisen not so much because behaviourism is wrong, but because there are aspects of human learning that it explains insufficiently. Cognitive theories, for example, seek to explain the higher-order processes of human thinking, while social theories expand on the opportunities to learn afforded by interaction between people. Such theories may be seen as developments of behaviourism, not incontrovertible objections.

Reinforcement is the key feature of the behavioural theories, and a reinforcer is anything that strengthens the desired response. It could be verbal praise, a good test result or a feeling of increased accomplishment or satisfaction. Reinforcers may be positive or negative. A positive reinforcer works when it is presented; a negative reinforcer works when it is withdrawn. Negative reinforcement is not punishment. Reinforcers always strengthen behaviour; that is what 'reinforced' means. Punishment is used to suppress behaviour. It consists of removing a positive reinforcer or presenting a negative one.

The behavioural approach has been applied widely in clinical settings (for modification of patient behaviour) and in schooling (for classroom management) as well as in adult education. Its effect has been felt most keenly in the field of school education, where the present focus on observable and measurable behaviour that can be staged, monitored and changed – in short scientifically controlled learning – can be traced back to behavioural theory. This approach is not concerned with the transmission of knowledge, nor with reflection on personal experience; similarly it is not concerned with the search for meaning and identity through social practice. It is concerned with primed and objective repetition of behaviours.

Consider the implications of reinforcement theory with regard to the development of skills. Practice takes the form of question (stimulus)–answer (response) frames that expose the learner to the topic in gradual steps. The learner is conditioned to make a response each time and receives immediate feedback. Learning is ordered in stages of difficulty so that the response to each step is likely to be correct; thus offering opportunities for positive reinforcement. Progress is achieved in small incremental steps and is 'shaped' towards a positive outcome. Skinner describes how a uniquely human form of reinforcement, verbal *instruction*, can be used to accelerate skills development:

A person learning to drive a car responds to the verbal behavior of the person sitting beside him; he starts, stops, shifts, signals, and so on when told to do so. These verbal stimuli may be at first directions, but they become instruction if verbal help is given out only as needed. The driver's behavior is then eventually taken over by the natural, nonverbal contingencies of driving a car. To learn to drive simply through exposure to those contingencies would take a very long time…By following instructions, he avoids exposure to many of these contingencies and eventually behaves as the instructor himself behaves. (Skinner 1974: 120–21.)

Skinner does not see this process in terms of the transmission of knowledge:

The instructor has not 'communicated' his knowledge or experience to the learner. The final uninstructed behavior is shaped and maintained by the natural contingencies of car and highway. The instructor has made it possible for the learner to come under their control speedily and without harm. (Skinner 1974: 121.)

Instruction is very much alive in skills and technical training programmes, professional development and all kinds of events that focus on the expert presenter. A vast range of techniques is available to reinforce behaviours, from conventional verbal delivery through to sophisticated web-based instructional design, and through varying mixes of reward and punishment. The classic 'chalk and talk' lecture even remains the cornerstone of teaching in higher education, though it is used less so now in schools. The stimulus–response mechanism can be seen as a major plank in many of these approaches to learning; so much so that training is perceived by many to be synonymous with instruction.

For decades, behavioural theorists have been excited by the possibilities of programmed instruction – the transmission of content in an orderly, thoughtful sequence by a machine (or indeed a purpose-designed book). The idea has its origins in work by Edward Thorndike and Sidney Pressey, but was extended and popularised by Skinner in the form of his 'teaching machine'. The basic component of the teaching machine was a program (software, in modern terminology) which led people through a series of instructions, questions and tasks (Hill 1990). A clear and linear link exists between such machines and the development of modern computer-based training (CBT), itself now eclipsed by web-based training (see Chapter 4: How different is e-learning?). Early machines made use of teaching and test items designed to shape behaviour through an orderly progression from the familiar to the unfamiliar aspects of a topic, in small stages, and using reinforcement to embed and encourage learning. They demonstrated greater efficiency and speedier responses than processes built around printed workbooks, but did not differ in qualitative terms.

Application

In dividing learning opportunities into those experienced *for* work, *at* work and *through* work, behaviour modification may be achieved in any or all of these situations. For example, vocational courses that lead to qualifications *for* work, and shorter courses designed to boost skills or increase professional status, often employ feedback and reinforcement processes, among other techniques. They succeed by priming the individual to behaviours that will make them more effective in work, and by identifying resources for continued development. Behaviourally oriented approaches can also be observed *at* work during many coaching sessions, one-to-one tuitions or, indeed, any instructor-led training activity. *Through* work, the characteristic application of behavioural theory is the formal direction and feedback of staff. A further example is apprenticeship, and other forms of supported practice ('sitting by Nelly'), in which instruction occurs during the course of an actual work task. Although less common over the past 30 years, the model of supported practice and detailed feedback is still maintained in highly vocational professions such as nursing and surgery, relying in part on instruction to reinforce and refine observed techniques. Table 1 summarises

how the behavioural approach is applied, together with a range of typical examples.

Key dilemmas

There is no doubt that behavioural reinforcement has an important, even unique, role in expediting learning. The key question is whether learning in such a manner out of context in a classroom results in learning directly, or whether it acts primarily as a stimulus to other learning processes. In the main, instruction tends to be a discontinuous activity inserted into busy working lives in a 'just in case' or 'just in time' manner. Its effects cannot easily be disentangled from other learning processes that the employee is undergoing concurrently, even if they are not aware. For example, important social learning may occur in and around the instruction episode (see Learning as social practice): discussion with colleagues before and after the episode may help the person to digest new ideas (see Learning as knowledge construction); and personal reflection may help to integrate new knowledge with existing structures (see Learning as understanding). Above all, experimentation and practice with new ideas immediately following the episode can help to ground them in personal and group

Table 1 | Learning as behaviour – approaches and examples

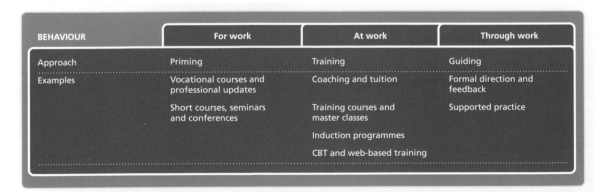

BEHAVIOUR	For work	At work	Through work
Approach	Priming	Training	Guiding
Examples	Vocational courses and professional updates	Coaching and tuition	Formal direction and feedback
	Short courses, seminars and conferences	Training courses and master classes	Supported practice
		Induction programmes	
		CBT and web-based training	

experiences. The familiar question, 'if all that you know was acquired during training courses, how much would you know?', has meaning because instruction cannot deliver learning effectively by itself: the fuller social, cognitive and experiential context of learning must be engaged.

A particular dilemma with programmed instruction is that its focus on correct responses to fixed circumstances does not support the transferability of skills from one situation to another, nor assist with the understanding of total situations. By definition, 'generic' content cannot be relevant to all situations; equally, content that is matched exactly to one task may be short-lived and inflexible in terms of skills acquisition. Again, recognition that instruction is a stimulus to learning, rather than its sole source, suggests a strategy of intertwining instruction with other forms of learning process, notably work practice.

A further dilemma emerges when we consider the unequal roles and power relationships of the novice and the expert. The suggestion that there is only ever 'one answer' and that it is known or not known can act as a brake on creativity and self-expression. Dependency on expert guidance, and derision of personal knowledge, are possible outcomes – perfect inhibitors of self-directed learning. In reality, the knowledge available to an individual and their associates may be extremely rich and more applicable to problem-solving than instruction originating from external sources.

Learning as understanding
Overview

This cluster of theories – also known as the cognitive learning theories – stresses the active involvement of the mind in learning. Responses are seen not as conditioned reactions to incoming stimuli, but thoughtful products of perceptions, beliefs and understandings. Learning is held to be a process of understanding the world, and of responding to it appropriately through a process of internalising its principles, concepts and facts. Vastly more complex mental activity is assumed than stimulus-response frames, resulting in the construction, reconstruction and, as necessary, deconstruction of mental models.

Theories of cognition regard the learner as a powerful information-processing machine whose task is to internalise knowledge about the world. Although the learner is in a position to vary the learning process, they are effectively enslaved to that task, obtaining feedback on their progress through the manipulation, testing and use of the knowledge so gained. Various theorists have attempted to highlight the key stages of cognitive development that fulfil this task, not least Benjamin S. Bloom's taxonomy of educational objectives (1956), Robert M. Gagné's conditions of learning (1966) and Jean Piaget's early development stages (1963), all of which remain fundamental to the design and assessment of education. Gagné's arrangement, for example, involves a sequence of increasingly complex cognitive stages, beginning at the lowest reaches with signal reception and stimulus-response behaviours, and proceeding to concept learning, principle learning and problem-solving at the highest level.

Piaget (1950) characterised the growth of knowledge in individuals as the interplay between two complementary processes. The first, known as *assimilation*, involves the integration of perceptions into a person's existing mental models, serving to confirm beliefs or explain novelty in familiar terms. The second, known as *accommodation*, involves the alteration of the

> 'Whereas assimilation may be interpreted as the person acting on the world, accommodation is the world acting on the person...'

models to explain perceptions which cannot otherwise be understood. Whereas assimilation may be interpreted as the person acting on the world, accommodation is the world acting on the person (Tennant 1997). Piaget viewed learning as the movement towards an equilibrium state characterised by coherent mixes of strategies and rules that explain the world. At different stages in the person's life, principally during childhood, the equilibrium states undergo a qualitative change leading to major advancements in understanding.

The search for equilibrium also features in Leon Festinger's (1957) theory of *cognitive dissonance*, which explains how people reconcile experiences that are at odds with their mental models. Festinger held that people will reduce the level of 'dissonance' in such situations by seeking consistency among their beliefs. This might require one of two things: a change in attitude or belief, or a change in behaviour. When faced with alternative options, he proposed that people would follow the line of least resistance, normally through an attitudinal change. The value of cognitive theories in explaining human development is apparent here. Such changes could not be explained so readily in terms of behaviourist-style reinforcement.

Cognitive development strategies place great emphasis on the process of *facilitation*, whereby the novice is helped to 'acquire understanding' through appropriate and efficient exposure to learning materials, and to solve given problems through 'guided search'. Good facilitation is expected to accelerate the novice through the developmental stages necessary to achieve mastery of the topic concerned (for example Bloom's or Gagné's stages). Since levels of individual understanding will vary significantly across the group, the facilitator needs to be aware of the

differences and to proceed incrementally from an acceptable starting point. 'Scaffolded' learning can be employed to structure and solidify understanding.

Large bodies of knowledge may be rendered digestible by subdivision into an ordered set of blocks (the curriculum) through which the learner proceeds under their own direction in self-study models, or through the help of a facilitator or instructor. CBT and web-based training offer scope for extensive learner control over pace, linearity and style, providing the learner with options about how and what they learn at every point. The assumption remains the same, however, that the body of knowledge presented must be internalised by the learner in order for them to reach the next developmental stage. This can be a very efficient and appropriate mechanism for learning some skills and topics.

Application

Examples of the cognitive approach to learning *for*, *at* and *through* work are plentiful. The chief concern in applying the cognitive approach to learning *for* work is to ensure that the individual becomes literate in the topic. This is achieved by exposing the learner to reference materials (ie content) such as books, journals, magazines, videos and web links, and facilitating engagement as appropriate. *At* work, learning can be facilitated by enriching the employee's sphere of knowledge in areas of personal weakness or corporate significance. Discussion of case studies, lessons learned and exemplar projects can have the effect of inviting the employee to review and, if necessary, challenge their work assumptions. Applied to learning *through* work, the cognitive approach might involve support for *in situ* problem-solving. A combination of 'just in time' knowledge services (what you need to know, when you need it) and robust thinking frameworks can enable employees to operate at the reaches of their cognitive development. Table 2 summarises the cognitive approach together with a series of examples.

Key dilemmas

There is a risk that learning opportunities which overemphasise the internalisation of explicit knowledge will result in employees who 'know the facts' but cannot translate them into appropriate actions. Such people may display impressive domain knowledge and perform well at IQ tests, but may fail to perform competently in the work setting. In Ryle's terms, the employee's knowledge is biased in favour of *knowing that* rather than *knowing how*. Clearly, cognitive approaches need to ensure that newly acquired knowledge is grounded in activities (especially work practice) to ensure parallel development of competence. One way of achieving this is to blend cognitively inspired interventions with experiential learning techniques – simulations, games, role plays, action learning and live work – such that the full experiential learning cycle is encompassed (see Chapter 1: Dimensions of learning).

A related dilemma concerns assessment. If learning is the internalisation of publicly verifiable knowledge, surely it must be straightforward to assess the degree to which an individual has accomplished this task? Most people who have experienced formal written examinations will have noticed their tendency to assess memory recall rather than potential performance in real situations[2]. Because of the huge variations that exist between people in respect of their experience, understanding, beliefs, attitudes and opportunities, there is a risk that exams of this kind will correlate strongly with the degree of opportunity afforded to the learner, rather than their potential to perform in a job role. Variation in background produces different entry points on to the learning curve, and different speeds of travel.

In order to construct an effective assessment strategy one must begin by identifying the strengths and weaknesses of an individual, such that progress can be recognised, monitored and, as necessary, nurtured. Howard Gardner (1983) suggests that every person has a unique portfolio of intelligences in multiple domains[3], which makes the challenge of individual assessment even more demanding. Hence the work on assessment, appraisal, intelligence quotients (IQ), psychometric

Table 2 | Learning as understanding – approaches and examples

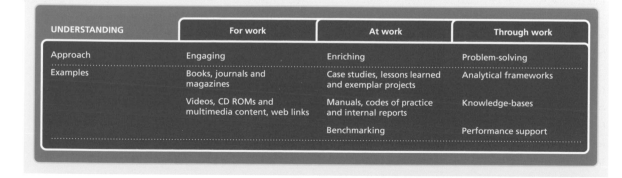

UNDERSTANDING	For work	At work	Through work
Approach	Engaging	Enriching	Problem-solving
Examples	Books, journals and magazines	Case studies, lessons learned and exemplar projects	Analytical frameworks
	Videos, CD ROMs and multimedia content, web links	Manuals, codes of practice and internal reports	Knowledge-bases
		Benchmarking	Performance support

'Dialogue is recognised to be one of the primary
vehicles for knowledge construction...'

testing, and so on, which has occupied
educationalists and psychologists for most of the
past century. If anything, this work has
demonstrated only that the concepts of
understanding and intelligence are hard to define;
that they vary according to the prior experience
and context of the individual in their work role;
and that no definitive method of assessment will
be applicable in all circumstances.

Work by Richard K. Wagner and Robert J.
Sternberg (1986) offers insight in this regard. They
reported only low correlations between
performance on IQ tests and in real-world settings,
about 20 per cent. Furthermore, their review of
the literature revealed that IQ tests are a better
predictor of training performance than job
performance by a factor of two. They concluded:

*That the tests predict training performance better
than job performance suggests that the tests
measure only a subset of the competencies
required for real-world success. (Wagner and
Sternberg 1986: 53.)*

This provides a link to the next cluster of learning
theories, which focuses on the activities of the
learner in real situations rather than their
intellectual achievements on paper.

Learning as knowledge construction
Overview

This cluster of theories holds that people are active
agents of their own learning, such that learning is
not separated from personal action. The approach
(following in the path of Dewey, Piaget and
Vygotsky) runs counter to the Platonic idea that
there is such a thing 'out there' as knowledge,
independent of the knower. Constructivists hold
that the only knowledge is personal knowledge (in
every respect tacit), and that learning does not

involve understanding the 'true' nature of things,
but is a personal construction of meaning out of
experience. The departure from cognitive theories
is clear: knowledge is a personal, subjective issue,
not an external commodity waiting to be
internalised through the absorption of content. In
a rebuttal of teaching methods that view the
learner as a passive recipient, Piaget said:

*Learning is possible only when there is active
assimilation. It is this activity on the part of the
subject which seems to me underplayed in the
stimulus-response schema...I think that without
this activity there is no possible didactic or
pedagogy which significantly transforms the
subject. (In: Campbell 1976: 77.)*

Constructivist theories are concerned
predominantly with social activity: learning is
believed to occur in dynamic interaction between
the individual and their environment. Social
context is crucial in this view of learning, since
individual thinking is shaped by active participation
in real situations. Because the approach links
learning so closely to personal experience, the act
of learning becomes inseparable from the
construction of meaning. Constructivists believe
that knowledge is usable by a person or group of
people only when it has meaning for them, ie
when it has arisen from their own experiences.
Hence the learner is placed at the centre of the
learning experience, rather than the expert
instructor (as in the behavioural approach) or the
content (as in the cognitive approach).

Dialogue is recognised to be one of the primary
vehicles for knowledge construction, hence
opportunities for discussion, debate and collective
analysis are seen as critical to the learning process.
In the teaching setting, the approach favours
hands-on, self-directed activities that lead to
debate, design and discovery. Constructivists

subscribe to the idea that learners *use* explicit knowledge and interaction with other people to construct their own understanding of the world, rather than present themselves as empty vessels to be filled. A recurrent theme is self-control – respect is shown for personal autonomy, self-direction and, ultimately, self-efficacy. Radical constructionists believe that 'tell and listen' forms of instruction damage the learner by denying them opportunities to construct knowledge for themselves (Rogers 1996).

As with the cognitive theories, there is general recognition that learning can be enhanced through facilitation. The task of the facilitator differs, however. It is not to advise the learner how to find creative methods of internalising content; it is to inspire the learner to discover knowledge for themselves. Carl R. Rogers (1961; 1983), one of the pioneers of the humanistic tradition of psychology, believed that you cannot teach a person directly; you can only facilitate their learning. Rogers placed particular emphasis on the formation of *dialogue* between the facilitator and participants in a learning experience and, by extension, between the participants themselves (see Chapter 3: The motivation to learn). Through dialogue, the facilitator helps to construct a shared understanding with and among the participants, producing powerful effects on capability and motivation (Senge 1990).

Facilitation involves creating an environment in which people can be stimulated to think and act beyond their current level of competence. It is important to identify activities that the learner cannot complete without the support of peers or reference materials. Ideally, participants should be involved in the formulation of problems as well as in the search for solutions (Eraut 1994); their role is to contribute ideas, listen to others, identify useful resources (intellectual, material, human),

and to evaluate the effort of themselves and the group. It is not uncommon for constructivist-inspired courses to operate without any formal content on the basis that the participants bring their own knowledge and experiences to the table.

Application

Devices that employ reflection such as personal and professional logs, or records of achievement, exemplify the constructivist approach in action *for* work. Some people are more adept and find greater value in this kind of activity than do others, but in recent years it has become a requirement in several professional circles, such as engineering and nursing. Supported online learning programmes also fall into this category (see Chapter 4: What is meant by e-learning?). Opportunities to construct new knowledge *at* work arise primarily through personal enquiry. When people conduct informal dialogues with mentors or managers, question and respond to colleagues, or talk to customers and suppliers, not only are ideas tested, accepted or rejected, but also behaviours, skills and relationships, producing a rich set of experiences on which to base understanding. Research projects and diagnostic exercises are equally processes of enquiry and discovery; research in particular develops the skills necessary for self-directed learning. Immersion holds the key to constructivist learning *through* work. Generating new knowledge is a natural outcome of creative work, but this can be accelerated by stepping into another employee's shoes or through participation in projects that demand significant new capabilities. Arguably, the immediacy and relevance of the situation makes this the most effective way of acquiring work-related understanding. Table 3 summarises the constructivist approach and provides a set of examples.

Key dilemmas

This cluster lays great stress on the context in which learning occurs. The potential for learning is thus mediated by a huge range of 'fuzzy' factors: the organisation, its people, its speed of change, and the level of support surrounding learners while learning is happening. The job function and the way it is organised are also critical: what opportunities do people have to co-operate with others, or to experiment with new ideas? All of these factors – physical, professional, psychological and social – will exert an influence on what is learned, creating new subtleties for training and development practitioners.

The radical nature of constructivism suggests that all knowledge is personally constructed and, thus, subjective. This doesn't negate explicit (codified) knowledge but does suggest that it will diffuse immediately into personal perspective and opinion. In order to control what and how people learn more tightly, trainers could adopt a more behavioural or cognitive-based approach to the delivery of learning priorities. This strategy doesn't come without risks, however. No matter how ubiquitous a message becomes, there is no guarantee that it will be accepted; likewise, a

policy that requires people to learn in just one fashion ('one shoe fits all') may inhibit some learning styles (see Chapter 3: Learning styles). The constructivist solution to this problem would be to align personal and organisational goals at the highest level, such that the needs of the person and the organisation overlap. The aim would be to unlock personal commitment and, with it, the drive to learn in mutually beneficial ways. Adjustments to the organisation's purpose, values or style of business might be necessary to achieve this.

If, as constructivists believe, all meaning is personal, then no concept can be taken as given without due personal understanding. This means that in every meeting, project or other business activity, little consistency of thought can be assumed across the group, especially when it contains people of varying age, sex, culture and background. The pursuit of shared vision under such circumstances can be a lengthy affair; there is also a possibility that misunderstanding or even conflict may arise in the absence of facilitation. Under the right circumstances, the interplay of perspectives can act as an amplifier of learning, making the investment of time and facilitation worthwhile. There remains no doubt, however,

Table 3 | Learning as knowledge construction – approaches and examples

KNOWLEDGE CONSTRUCTION	For work	At work	Through work
Approach	Reflecting	Enquiring	Immersing
Examples	Personal and professional logs	Mentoring	Special projects
	Records of achievement and portfolios	Brainstorming, knowledge sharing and workshops	Job rotations and secondments
	Supported online learning	Discussions with colleagues, customers, suppliers	
		Diagnostic tools	

that constructivist training interventions are more challenging to manage and less easily scaled. There is no constructivist equivalent to the packed lecture hall, or the CBT experience distributed to thousands of employees.

Learning as social practice
Overview

As an adjunct to the previous theories, social theories of learning locate learning in the process of co-operation. They don't contradict the idea of individual cognition or knowledge construction occurring in the head of an individual, nor the fact that behavioural mechanisms may be at work in conditioning many human behaviours, but they argue that learning requires a social setting to occur, and to be applied. Indeed, authors such as Vygotsky (1978), Lave and Wenger (1991), Engestrom and Middleton (1996) maintain that learning is either an outcome of social interaction or an integral and inseparable aspect of social practice.

As we saw in Chapter 1, the origin of the idea can be traced back to Vygotsky, who observed that children could perform well above their mental age if provided with elementary assistance by an adult or older child. He used the phrase *zone of proximal development* to describe the extension, in years, that the child was able to exhibit in proximity and empathy with others. Think of a brainstorming session, and how much more can be gained from several people sharing their ideas. The scaffolding effect of social interaction ('the whole is greater than the sum of its parts') will be familiar to many.

Based on these early experiments, Vygotsky concluded that social interaction is an inseparable part of learning about certain forms of know-how.

The example he gave was cultural development:

Every function of the child's cultural development appears twice: first, on the social level, and later, on the individual level; first, between *people* (interpsychological)*, and then* inside *the child* (intrapsychological). *Vygotsky 1978: 57.*

Extrapolated to other forms of know-how, it is easy to see why the idea of learning being primarily a social phenomenon has exercised such attraction (contributions to the field have emerged from anthropology, sociology, social psychology and cognitive science). The key point is that social context is crucial for effective learning, since individual thinking is shaped by active participation in real situations.

Social learning theories take numerous different forms. *Cognitive–social theories* (for example Bandura 1977) view learning as the outcome of a series of information-processing steps in the brain set in train by social interactions, leading to imitation, emulation and adaptive behaviour. *Activity theories* (for example Engestrom and Middleton 1996) view established patterns of social interaction as the source of learning at work. Interaction between people is held to be the primary phenomenon, with learning as one of its outcomes. The resolution of inconsistencies and tensions arising within (and between) activity systems during participation in recurrent and embedded activities is held by activity theorists to be the chief agent of learning (Blackler *et al* 1999).

Lave and Wenger (1991) approach learning from yet another perspective, viewing it as the normal outcome of social practice. Their theory, known as *situated learning*, asserts that learning takes place through *legitimate peripheral participation*: legitimate in the sense that interaction is socially approved; peripheral because it happens unavoidably and incidentally; and participatory because that is what social action is about. Learning is therefore distributed among co-participants in a community of practice, and knowledge is embedded within it. Newcomers acquire, through participation, a sense of how people act in relation to tasks and towards each other; in doing so they become members of the community themselves:

Viewing learning as legitimate peripheral participation means that learning is not merely a condition for membership, but is itself an evolving form of membership. We conceive of identities as long-term, living relations between persons and their place and participation in communities of practice. Thus identity, knowing and social membership entail one another. (Lave and Wenger 1991: 53.)

Wenger (1998) suggests that we *all* participate in communities of practice – some recognised less well than others – and that these are our primary sources of learning, if not its mental apparatus. We shall at any one time be old-timers in some communities and newcomers in others; apprentices in some while masters in others. Social participation results in all members of the community learning, and while the apprentice might be the one who is changed most, the master also changes through their role as co-learner. Chris Collison and Geoff Parcell (2001: 127) identify three types of community operating in a large energy company:

1   Communities of interest: groups of people who have common interest in a particular topic or activity, often outside work. Examples include sports and hobby clubs, good causes, and social associations.

2   Communities of practice: groups that participate in the same type of practices and demonstrate a common understanding of methods, including how and when to apply them. Described by the authors as 'guardians of competence in that practice within the company', they stress their ability to *enable* work.

3   Communities of commitment: groups that are accountable for delivering specific business goals. Dynamic structures that may fold when the project is delivered, the authors note their 'much harder edge' than communities of practice.

The idea that participation in a working environment can lead to learned behaviour has been described engagingly by Donald Roy (1959). His article, entitled 'Banana Time', concerned a group of people working in the 'clicking room' of a clothing factory, learning to remain sane in the face of repetitive work. An identity emerged among the group which gave meaning to the routine tasks. In one sense the participants were working for each other rather than the factory, with positive motivational effects.

Application

Collison and Parcell's three types of community – interest, practice and commitment – correspond roughly to the categories of analysis used in this chapter to assess learning theories, namely learning *for*, *at* and *through* work. The significance of social practice in supporting learning *for* work is illustrated by the popularity of professional bodies, interest groups and alumni associations to which individuals may belong throughout their careers. In Britain, such bodies developed their own forms of training and certification ahead of universities,

> **'Participation in both informal and formal communities
> serves to negotiate purpose in work activities; shared vision,
> identity and meaning among the group may follow.'**

giving practitioners exclusive responsibility for training new entrants through periods of apprenticeship[4]. The structures that remain – royal colleges, learned societies, professional institutes – are now hubs of professional development and networking.

The value of personal networks and communities of practice to learning *at* work is indisputable, as well more formalised structures and groupings that bring cross-sections of employees closer together. Participation in both informal and formal communities serves to negotiate purpose in work activities; shared vision, identity and meaning among the group may follow. Participation also provides a systemic mechanism for brainstorming, innovation and standard-setting. Social learning, it seems, acts as an important enabling factor in the workplace.

Teams have legendary ability to deliver projects; their parallel role in fuelling learning *through* work is less obvious, but equally compelling. The extent to which the team itself adds to the total knowledge constructed by its members depends on its purpose, time span, diversity, organisation and the range of tasks undertaken. Whatever its

form – and there are many – new knowledge is very likely to emerge from the experience. Table 4 summarises the socially mediated approach to learning, together with examples of typical methods.

Key dilemmas

Organisational culture is a factor determining the degree and transparency with which people interact, and the degree to which social learning is possible. Harvard Professor of Education and Organizational Behavior, Chris Argyris, reminds us that everything done in the organisation is underpinned by a constantly shifting cultural order manifested in stories, symbols and power structures. This results in a moving set of traditions, values, policies, beliefs and attitudes; a multi-faceted organism drawing on the collective energies of everybody involved, constantly seeking to interpret and reinterpret itself.

The extent to which shared understanding can be reached in such an environment is problematic. Michael Eraut talks about the 'crowdedness' of a situation, and the difficulty of communicating effectively amongst the cut-and-thrust of everyday

Table 4 | Learning as social practice – approaches and examples

SOCIAL PRACTICE	For work	At work	Through work
Approach	Networking	Participating (in communities)	Teamworking
Examples	Professional bodies	Personal networks	Project teams
	Committees, boards and advisory groups	Communities of practice	Functional teams
	Interest groups and associations	Internal committees and management groups	Multi-disciplinary teams
	Alumni associations	Action learning sets	Virtual or distributed teams
			Multi-organisation teams

activity. Think about the modern classroom or shop floor, and imagine the extent to which meaningful interaction might occur, and hence meaningful learning. Stories have a particular significance here in binding together complex and sometimes uncertain sequences of events in a communicable form. They are themselves dynamic, politically spun, and responsive to circumstances (Boje 1991).

The ability of a person to learn through social practice must also depend on their personal disposition and social skills. We rarely choose the people we work with, yet our familiarity with those around us must influence how successfully we interact with them and, consequently, learn. Given so many contingencies, can socially anchored learning ever amount to more than an *ad hoc* set of interactions? To the extent that this question assumes that learning should be an orderly, controlled experience, drawing on a defined curriculum and working toward a fixed objective, the answer has to be no. As a driver of informal learning in organisations, however, its potential exceeds all other theories.

Conclusion

Approaches to learning are many, and this chapter has attempted to cover the contributions of most

significance to workplace learning. To help reflect on the large number of ways that learning may be realised, and on the variety of resources and methods available to training and development practitioners, the discussion has been organised into the 4 x 3 matrix shown in Table 5.

The theories each have strengths and weaknesses and, in describing their particular foci, it is worth bearing in mind the need to consider fitness-for-purpose when planning learning. The most positive outcomes are likely to occur when learning is linked directly to the job function, and opportunities are provided for the immediate application of new-found capabilities. Put simply, however, behavioural approaches are probably best suited to developing skills, cognitive approaches to increase knowledge, constructivist approaches to enhance performance, and socially mediated learning to accelerate change. In any particular situation, a mix of all four approaches might result in the best overall programme – richness of process is the key.

Table 6 summarises the primary focus of each theory cluster; if you like, its centre of gravity. Neighbouring columns indicate the process by which learning is assumed to take place, and the outcomes that are possible. In reality, each of the approaches could lead to any of the outcomes, but

Table 5 | Summary of approaches to learning by cluster

	For work	At work	Through work
Behaviour	Priming	Training	Guiding
Understanding	Engaging	Enriching	Problem-solving
Knowledge construction	Reflecting	Enquiring	Immersing
Social practice	Networking	Participating (in communities)	Teamworking

there remains a sense that reinforcement is most easily assessed in terms of skills development; internalisation through displays of knowledge; activities through work performance; and group practice in terms of the extent to which it has enabled change.

Successful application of almost any learning theory depends on the existence of a conducive physical, psychological and social environment in the organisation. The ramifications of this issue form the subject of the next chapter.

Endnotes

1 Other significant contributors in this field have been E.F. Thorndike and S. Markle.

2 The value of the exam lies in its ability to quality-assure a person's academic potential in the eyes of society.

3 Gardner's multiple intelligences are linguistic, logical-mathematical, spatial, musical, bodily-kinaesthetic, interpersonal, intrapersonal, naturalist and, possibly, existential intelligence.

4 Barristers professionalised in the thirteenth century, physicians in the sixteenth, solicitors and surgeons in the eighteenth, and engineers in the nineteenth centuries.

Table 6 | Summary of approaches to learning by focus, process and outcome

	Focus	Process	Outcome
Behaviour	The expert	Reinforcement	Skills
Understanding	The content	Delivery	Knowledge
Knowledge construction	The learner	Activity	Performance
Social practice	The group	Practice	Change

3 | Learning in practice

When I was a boy of 14, my father was so ignorant I could hardly stand to have the old man around. But when I got to be 21, I was astonished at how much the old man had learned in seven years.

Mark Twain, 1835–1910

◘ **Learning is deeply affected by the context in which it occurs. As well as the specific nature of the learning experience itself, contributing factors include organisational culture, support for learners, employee motivation, and the physical environment.**

◘ **Motivation is both a determinant and an outcome of achievement. In the right context, and with effective support and reward mechanisms, learning can motivate staff by enhancing their ability to achieve goals.**

◘ **Learners have characteristic strengths and preferences in the ways they take in and process information, known as learning styles. Learners are not fixed in one style and will benefit from exposure to a full range of approaches.**

Learning theories are an important, if sometimes neglected, piece of the training and development puzzle. The framework presented in the previous chapter aimed to address this by defining what is common in human learning. The intention was to shed light on the traditions that gave rise to the theories, as well as their interrelationships, in order to help practitioners to distinguish between fundamental and incremental change in their profession, and to appraise new ideas constructively.

Yet theoretical approaches are by no means sufficient in themselves to guide implementation. Even the most theoretically robust methods must take account of the different ways in which people respond to learning opportunities. Some of the factors known to affect engagement in learning and, hence, to influence the translation of theory into practice, include: the climate for learning,

employee motivation, the physical environment, and learning styles.

This chapter explores each of these areas in turn from both theoretical and practical standpoints, in particular their degree of influence over learning effectiveness. An important question for practitioners is this: what factors can be managed, and what may only be encouraged?

The climate for learning
Overview

Success in facilitating learning at work depends on the organisation's ability to understand where it lies in the external environment, how it needs to adapt to changing conditions, and how it should go about encouraging new patterns of behaviour – all of this on a continuing basis and in a way that engages the full workforce. There is general

'...the inducement to learn is much more likely to originate at the level of a small, active group than from remoter sources of management.'

agreement that the capability to adapt will be constrained by the structure of the organisation, determined by its history, size, objectives and people (Schein 1980; Handy 1985; Argyris 1994) and by the extent to which these are understood internally, and addressed in decision-making:

An organisation's health and effectiveness will depend ultimately upon its ability to diagnose its own problems and to develop its own solutions. (Schein 1980: 35.)

Because organisations are complex social systems, their study entails examining the behaviour of multiple groups, agents and sub-systems, all of which are subject to internal and external pressures. Progression towards ever more responsive and flexible workforces is edging organisations in the direction of new levels of psychological contract with their employees, new management approaches and an expectation of continuous change. This section explores two factors that set the tone for learning in an organisation – its culture and the level of support for learning offered to employees.

Organisational culture

Argyris (1994) draws attention to the ever-present rules, rituals and assumptions in an organisation that influence the way people behave. Spoken or unspoken, formal or informal, heeded or ignored, such rules define the culture of the organisation. Organisational metaphors abound – business as war, the organisation as machine, the CEO as ship's captain, the unit as a community – and the way that this is played out affects the degree of learning that is possible. If, for example, the machine metaphor is in favour, we expect rationality, objectivity, and automated production lines that must not be held up. Carried further, this

may encourage downplaying of individual contributions, Marxian alienation, and a culture of blame and accountability. There is not much likelihood of learning, or indeed sharing of information, in such an environment.

On the other hand, sustained interaction between members of a formal or informal group can create shared values and identity among its members from which strong feelings of loyalty arise. As Wenger describes, the inducement to learn is much more likely to originate at the level of a small, active group than from remoter sources of management:

Workers organise their lives with their immediate colleagues and customers to get their jobs done. In doing so, they develop or preserve a sense of themselves they can live with, have some fun, and fulfil the requirements of their employers and clients. No matter what their official job description may be, they create a practice to do what needs to be done. Although workers may be contractually employed by a large institution, in day-to-day practice they work with – and, in a sense, for – a much smaller set of people. (Wenger 1998: 6.)

Cultures that value the contributions of small, self-sustaining groups also demonstrate that they value diversity, differences of perspective and alternative ideas. By giving currency to diversity, innovation and learning can be supported.

In terms of how a culture might be changed, work by Argyris and Schön (1974; 1978) is significant. They proposed that any person will articulate an *espoused theory* to describe and justify their behaviour, and which is assumed to guide their activities. Underlying this theory will be their *theory in use*, as evidenced by their actual practice, and the two will differ:

When someone is asked how he would behave under certain circumstances, the answer he usually gives is his espoused theory of action for that situation. This is the theory of action to which he gives allegiance, and which, upon request, he communicates to others. However, the theory that actually governs his actions is his theory-in-use. (Argyris and Schön 1974: 6–7.)

Clearly, espoused theories of an organisation are how it *wishes* to be perceived, and how it *says* that it behaves, compared to what is actually *done*. How many times have we observed a gap between what an organisation says of itself and what is clear from everyday evidence? Bringing these two together is the primary concern of what Argyris (1976) described as 'double loop' learning, the process of questioning the assumptions underlying current views in a public fashion, in order to encourage fundamental enquiry, learning and change. The risk with more superficial fixes is that the gap between real and espoused is never closed, leading to an erosion of enthusiasm – indeed reason – to learn (Argyris 1998).

Support for learning

The experiential nature of learning presents something of a challenge for many organisations: if learning is embedded in work, then it must occur in a highly decentralised fashion. What, then, is the role of the training and development practitioner? Increasingly they may find themselves serving as supporters and facilitators of learning rather than as providers of outside knowledge; instituting processes that tap into individual and group knowledge rather than organising training courses; and identifying learning communities in order to support them more effectively. Recent work by Martin, Pate and Beaumont exposes the paradox behind this last objective:

Although communities of practice are informal and self-organising, paradoxically management, perhaps in conjunction with educators, should learn how to identify potential communities of practice; provide an infrastructure that will support them, including budgets and access to formal learning through the methods of, say, action learning; and use non-traditional methods to assess the values of communities of practice, by gathering data on members' stories of the complex relationships between work, learning and performance. (Martin et al 2001.)

There is a lot involved in perfecting a learning facilitation strategy: physical proximity of staff does not guarantee diffusion of knowledge, less still spontaneous formation of communities. Furthermore, conventional views of training still abound, and support for the self-directed learner, and for the communities of practice that they utilise and sustain, may not be recognised as a priority by the training and development function. Yet, if anything, the value of non-conventional learning support increases with the overall pace of business practice; spiralling competition and uncertainties in markets mean that more and more employees will grow to depend on their personal and group initiative, and less so on external, reactive interventions.

The role of the training practitioner becomes more complex with every new factor that is taken into account: culture, trust, motivation and learning style all come into play, not just in respect of individuals but of groups. The role of the middle manager is crucial in this respect since they can inspire learning among junior colleagues in a variety of ways:

1   They can attempt to create a positive climate for learning, to combat the feeling that it is intruding on work.

2   They can offer guidance on purpose, highlighting the links between learning activities and business objectives.

3   They can provide access to learning resources, external opportunities and people, including training and development professionals.

4   They can help to create opportunities for employees to test out and consolidate their learning.

5   They can provide regular and constructive feedback on learning and performance.

Regrettably, middle managers are not always judged or assisted in their attempts to assist learning at work. This raises the possibility of a serious knock-on effect on junior staff, since the attitudes they absorb from middle managers may shape their own approaches to learning.

The motivation to learn
Overview

The disposition and commitment of the learner – their motivation to learn – is one of the most critical factors influencing learning effectiveness. Under the right conditions, a strong disposition to learn, enhanced by solid experience and a positive attitude, can lead to exceptional performance. Yet it is difficult to be certain about cause and effect here. An independent spirit provided with the opportunity to tackle meaningful challenges can be highly receptive to learning, but what comes first, the attitude or the opportunity?

The motivation to learn may be defined as those factors that energise and direct behavioural patterns organised around a learning goal (Rogers 1996). As such, it joins other forms of motivation

in depending on a wide range of influences, from the desire to meet essential needs to the instinctive pleasure of solving problems. Intense research of these and other drivers of motivation has resulted in a succession of theories, all of which suggest that motivation plays a pivotal role in learning.

Extrinsic and intrinsic factors

Motivation may be separated into two sets of factors. *Extrinsic* factors originate in external structures and rewards, including pay and conditions, professional standards, organisational policies and norms, as well as requirements originating in formal learning programmes where the individual is enrolled. *Intrinsic* factors stem from inner or self-driven pressures to grow and achieve, and thus include personal desires, the need to conform, the quest for esteem, and instinctive urges to solve problems and support other people. Alignment of intrinsic and extrinsic motivation, if possible, would create the ideal conditions for workplace achievement, since employee and organisation would be motivated by the same objectives.

Extrinsic sources of motivation change throughout the course of an individual's life as they pursue different activities, take on different roles, and associate with different social and professional groups. In contrast, intrinsic sources of motivation are usually more stable since they are intertwined with the person's whole experience and identity. An example might be the motivation of participants within a programme of study leading towards a qualification. Course managers will be aware that some participants engage in strategies designed to limit effort while maximising the likelihood of passing examinations – so called 'surface' learning strategies (Morgan 1993). Such strategies bypass the extrinsic reason for running the course, which is to develop employee capability across the curriculum, but answer the intrinsic desires of participants for visibility in the job marketplace.

Theories of motivation

Behaviourist theories of motivation tend to focus on extrinsic factors, especially rewards and punishments; set up an appropriate reward system and motivation will follow. Cognitive theories deal with intrinsic factors, in particular the formation of intentions and goal-seeking behaviours. Constructivist (also referred to as humanist or needs-based) theories emphasise the individual's desire for personal change, growth and responsibility, while social theories stress the search for meaning and identity among peers. All these views of motivation are complementary, and rather than attempt to cover the full range of ideas in this section, a selection has been made.

Maslow – satisfying essential needs

Abraham Maslow (1968) was a pioneer of the humanist or needs-based tradition in psychology and is best known for his arrangement of human needs, and hence motivations, into a simple hierarchy as illustrated in Figure 3. Maslow suggested that human beings are driven to satisfy each level of the hierarchy sequentially, beginning with food and shelter, and progressing on through safety, love, esteem to a state he referred to as 'self-actualisation' – the expression of creativity, the fulfilment of potential. The act of satisfying needs at one level is said to spark interest and attention in the next level up. While Maslow did speak about the hierarchy as if it were a fixed order, he appreciated that exceptions were possible and considered it to be more Utopian than rigid:

Figure 3 | Maslow's hierarchy of human needs

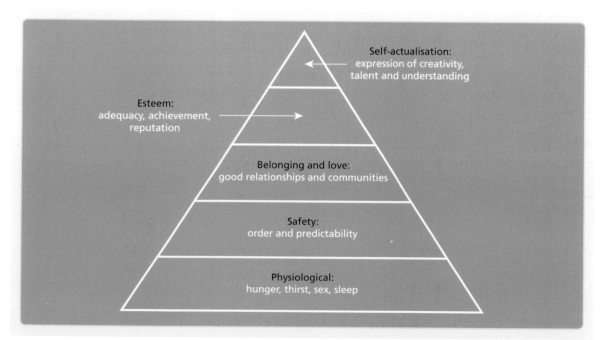

> ‘One of the most interesting aspects of Maslow's work is the notion that humans are programmed physiologically to self-actualise, and hence come equipped with the need to know.’

So far, our theoretical discussion may have given the impression that these five sets of needs – physiological, safety, belongingness, esteem, and self-actualization – are somehow in such terms as the following: If one need is satisfied, then another emerges. This statement might give the false impression that a need must be satisfied 100 percent before the next need emerges. In actual fact, most members of our society who are normal are partially satisfied in all their basic needs and partially unsatisfied in all their basic needs at the same time. (Maslow 1987: 26.)

Maslow's thinking was something of a breakthrough – most psychology before him had concentrated on patients who were abnormal or ill, whereas he wanted to understand the drivers of good mental health, of positive motivation. His work gave rise to forms of therapy that assume that people will use their in-built capability to learn and grow provided they are helped to overcome fears, pains and other anxieties. One of the most interesting aspects of Maslow's work is the notion that humans are programmed physiologically to self-actualise, and hence come equipped with the need to know. Environment and culture can alter the speed with which this takes place, but the pressure to know persists:

All those physical and social factors that increase fear will cut our impulse to know; all factors that permit courage, freedom and boldness will thereby also free our need to know. (Maslow 1968: 67.)

Rogers – the quest for responsibility

Carl R. Rogers (1961) was another early pioneer of the human-needs tradition in psychology. Like Maslow he also viewed motivation as the satisfaction of inner drives, but chose to emphasise the drive towards adulthood, responsibility and

independence. As indicated in Chapter 2, he saw learning as an integral part of this process and became convinced that one can only *facilitate* learning in another person, not teach them directly.

Rogers was a strong proponent of experiential and self-directed approaches to learning. He observed that people with an intrinsic need to know something will learn faster and more effectively than those being instructed out of context in a classroom. An example of this is software: a person is more likely to learn how to use a software application if they need it to perform a task (eg write their CV); learning without the need is unlikely to be effective. In *Freedom to Learn* (1983), Rogers describes the demotivating effect of ill-timed or irrelevant instruction, which he suggests engages only the brain, not the whole person[1]:

We frequently fail to recognize that much of the material presented to students in the classroom has, for the student, the same perplexing, meaningless quality that the list of nonsense syllables has for us…Thus, education becomes the futile attempt to learn material that has no personal meaning. (Rogers 1983: 19.)

He contrasts this with experiential learning:

When the toddler touches a warm radiator, she learns for herself the meaning of the word hot; she has learned a future caution in regard to all similar radiators; and she has taken in these learnings in a significant, involved way that will not soon be forgotten. (Rogers 1983: 19.)

In applying his experience of clinical psychology to education, Rogers pioneered the approach of listening to the particular issues, questions and problems that participants bring to an educational experience (Smith 1997). He prescribed a set of core conditions for facilitative practice designed to motivate people to learn (Rogers 1983: 121–6):

1   *Realness*, or the act of being physically present and forging genuine relationships with learners.

2   *Acceptance*, as in caring for the learner as a separate person, having worth in their own right.

3   *Empathetic understanding* of the learner from their own point of view, without evaluation or judgement.

In redefining the role of the teacher as a facilitator of learning, Rogers reminds us to hand over responsibility for learning to the employee, while cultivating the motivation to learn through appropriate involvement, support and praise. Malcolm Knowles (1980) formulated what was at the time a radical approach to adult education based upon this idea known as androgogy[2], or the 'art and science of helping adults learn'. Knowles cited seven processes designed to motivate self-directed learning, which were later extended by Mezirow (1983) into a 'charter for androgogy'; Tennant (1997) also proposed a further version of the charter. As the benefits of self-directed learning become more widely recognised by educators, it is fair to say that the greatest legacy of androgogy is its charters (Tight 1996).

Expectancy theory

The role of expectancy in motivating employees was first presented in coherent theoretical terms by Victor H. Vroom (1964), and was later expanded into a comprehensive theory by Kenneth

W. Howard (1989). Vroom held that motivation cannot be explained simply in terms of the needs people are trying to fulfil: the central problem is how to explain the *choices* they make between alternative sets of behaviours. He proposed that people, when deciding how to act, estimate the likelihood that they will achieve the task (expectancy), what outcomes might result (instrumentality), and how desirable these outcomes are to them (valency):

Whenever an individual chooses between alternatives which involve uncertain outcomes, it seems clear that his behaviour is affected not only by his preferences, but also by the degree to which he believes these outcomes to be probable. (Vroom 1964: 17.)

An example of how expectancy and valency combine is the lottery ticket. No one would argue that the potential outcome is significant, nor that its valency is very high. The decision therefore rests on the individual's expectancy of success; even a low expectancy may be sufficient to purchase a ticket, but zero expectancy would not. An important question for training and development practitioners is how to increase the valency of training and learning experiences, and how to build the expectancy that they will succeed.

The essence of expectancy theory is that people act in ways that are likely to benefit them *based upon the expected results of their actions* (Crowder and Pupynin 1993). Behaviour is driven by the expectation of achievement, a connection which is reinforced when the expectation is well founded. The model holds that motivation, in particular job satisfaction, is an *outcome* of achievement, not the other way around, such that the two feed off each other in a virtuous circle. As an agent of achievement, learning plays a key role in sustaining a positive performance expectancy.

Goal theory

Goals feature extensively in the study of motivation, in particular their difficulty, acceptance, specificity and proximity. Goals are not the same as tasks: they refer to the objects or aims of particular actions, not to rich and multifaceted problems. This distinction is necessary in order to understand the impact of goal *difficulty* on performance. The research evidence is clear that performance is correlated very highly with goal difficulty, harder goals inciting greater interest, commitment and effort than easier ones (Locke *et al* 1981)[3]. Bandura puts it like this:

The higher the performance standards people set for themselves, the greater their attainments are likely to be. High achievers tend to make self-satisfaction contingent upon attainment of difficult goals; low achievers adopt easy goals as sufficient. (Bandura 1977: 163.)

The relationship between performance and task difficulty is not so clear. In order to complete a task, specific skills, knowledge and resources may be necessary, and these may not be present in the individuals concerned. Tasks set beyond a person's reach, or that lack the necessary support structures, can be highly discouraging, especially when strong effort is required, or they occur frequently.

Predictably, goals must be *accepted* by a person for motivation to follow; those that are not felt to be in their basic interest may be resisted. This highlights the need to envisage tasks and set goals appropriate to the individual concerned (challenging, yes, but impossible, no) and to seek their involvement in goal-setting at an early stage. The need for employees to 'own' their behaviours comes up almost universally in motivation theories,

whether applied to training situations or more generally in work.

Goal *specificity* is a further area where the research evidence is clear. Vague goals like 'do your best' definitely inspire less action than those that are clear and unambiguous in their interpretation (Locke *et al* 1981). In fact, there would seem to be no advantage in issuing vague goals over issuing no goals at all:

We have not found any differences in the results obtained by studies in which no goals are assigned and those in which subjects are explicitly told to do their best. No goal subjects, it appears, try to do as well as they can on the assigned task. (Locke et al 1981: 129.)

Last, the effect of goal *proximity* on motivation can be extremely strong. Breaking down a distant goal into a series of smaller, proximate goals, each inducing motivation, action and reward, helps to sustain momentum that might otherwise be diffused. Bandura vividly describes the risks of dealing only in remote intentions:

Immediate goals mobilise effort and direct what one does in the here and now. Remote intentions are too far removed in time to serve as effective incentives for action, especially when there are many competing influences at hand, as is usually the case. By focusing on the distant future, it is easy to put off matters in the present – one can always begin in earnest tomorrow. (Bandura 1977: 162.)

To maintain motivation when confronted with distant goals, he suggests the formation of explicit proximate sub-goals that are instrumental in achieving larger future ones. Quite complex strategies may be built around this idea, involving

> **'...motivation is hard to manage since it is dependent on the whole person, not simply their presence as an employee.'**

dynamic planning and the adjustment of sub-goals based on critical appraisal of performance.

Bandura – self-regulation

One drawback of cognitive explanations of motivation (such as expectancy theory and goal theory) is that they do not focus sufficiently on the *social context* within which decisions are made. Bandura (1977; 1986) sought to address this by linking motivation to the pursuit of socially accepted standards of behaviour. He recognised that when people fall short of the standards of behaviour they wish to display, dissatisfactions occur which motivate action, learning and change. Unlike cognitive explanations, however, he suggests that it is not the expectation or reward that produces the motivational effect, it is the knowledge that people – for example colleagues or clients – will respond *evaluatively* to one's behaviour.

Motivation is seen as a process of self-regulation, creating the drive to meet socially accepted standards of performance as established by role models and embodied in tacit assumptions about ideal behaviour. Since formal and informal feedback on achievement is a regular feature of most jobs, the information necessary to measure personal performance and self-regulate is readily available.

Organisational responses

Four aspects of motivation are particularly significant for training and development practitioners. First, motivation is hard to manage since it is dependent on the whole person, not simply their presence as an employee. This means that even the most supportive team member or manager will be inherently restrained in their capacity to cultivate motivation in others. Beyond their reach will lie dependencies in the social, economic and cultural domains of the people concerned, areas that the organisation may lack the means or inclination to understand.

Second, the factors driving motivation are sensitive to space, time and context. Frederick Herzberg and his colleagues deduced in 1959 that the main factors that motivate employees are achievement, recognition, work itself, responsibility and advancement (Herzberg *et al* 1959; Herzberg 1968). The problem is that these factors are not durable: they arise and diminish in the context of specific tasks, conversations and times, and require constant reinforcement to be maintained. Furthermore, factors that create dissatisfaction and poor performance – Herzberg's so-called hygiene factors – tend to have longer-lasting effects on employees. Here he cited ineffectiveness or unfair policies of the organisation, poor supervision, low salaries, difficult interpersonal relationships, and unsatisfactory working conditions. Attempts to boost motivation must be accompanied by the removal of these demotivators if they are to stand much chance of success.

Third, if motivation is an outcome of achievement (as well as a determinant), organisations should attempt to create a positive expectancy of performance among all employees, not just high performers. This means investing in structures that support learning, communication, co-operation and problem-solving *in situ*, as well as via formal training interventions.

Fourth, it is possible only to facilitate learning in other people, not to teach them directly. This seemingly minor distinction masks a profound change in practice, described by Knowles as the transition from pedagogy (originally the art and science of teaching children) to androgogy (the art and science of facilitating learning in adults). In reality there is less value in separating child and adult education than Knowles proposed: there are no clear-cut boundaries, and both areas are moving in a similar direction. Creating a positive climate for learning; involving the person in all stages of their learning, including planning; supporting the learner emotionally, physically and intellectually; and progressively handing over responsibility for learning to the person, are generally accepted to inspire self-directed learning across all age groups.

The physical learning environment
Overview

The question of *where* to situate learning is a common concern of training and development practitioners. We know, for example, that the experience of leaving one's immediate work setting to attend a learning event can be extremely positive: the learner can step back from their challenges and, with fresh eyes, engage in reflective processes with other learners. We also know that a great deal of important learning occurs during work, immersed in activities and everyday office experiences. So, do the advantages of studying outside of the work setting outweigh the benefits of anchoring learning in work? Certainly, the logistical challenges of managing a purpose-built training facility are considerable and, if learning were to be effective in the office environment (or indeed in the field or at home), many costs could be saved. This section explores this dilemma from two different perspectives, that of training and learning.

Locating training

As we saw in Chapter 1, experiential learning is the transformation of experience into knowledge.

Kolb's cycle begins and ends with experience, interspersed with reflective, cognitive and experimentation processes. Time away from the office on a learning event provides the opportunity to reflect on personal experiences, and often results in fresh approaches to entrenched problems. Clearly, such benefits do not result automatically: their appearance depends on the provision of a supportive, unthreatening learning environment, and the use of learning processes that encourage learners to converse, reflect and, if necessary, 'unlearn' fixed patterns of behaviour. Learner disposition is also paramount.

Increasingly, learning can be brought to the learner, rather than the latter having to move physically to reach it. E-learning technologies such as streaming audio and video, group communication and virtual collaboration tools, allow features of the physical learning experience to be replicated on the desk-top or portable computer. While such experiences may lack the social capital generated by face-to-face contact, there is no doubt that virtual learning can be effective, fun and, in some cases, equally or more efficient (especially in time, travel and accommodation terms) than conventional face-to-face training[4].

Learning virtually, through a computer, does present some serious challenges, however. A recent questionnaire by the Masie Center found that 53 per cent of employees would prefer to participate in important e-learning activities somewhere other than at their desks, and that 50 per cent per cent of employees described the desk-based environment as distracting (Masie 2000). Having access to a private office obviously helps, but doors cannot prevent incoming telephone calls, e-mails and other forms of noise and interruption. Masie offered a series of tips on how to manage desk-based learning: door signs and other visual announcements, special-purpose learning spaces and laboratories, flexibility in home working arrangements, headsets, courses with in-built time allowances for other tasks, group working, and attention-grabbing content (Masie 2000: 3).

As desk-top training encounters the realities of office life, two issues emerge. First, the value of a quiet place to go for study and reflection remains undisputed by theoretical or practical research. Depending on the expected level of demand, a purpose-built facility may or may not be required. A lower-cost alternative is the provision of quiet areas equipped with relevant learning resources, analytical tools ('thinking frameworks') and Internet connections. Where a suitable domestic environment exists, home learning may also be encouraged. Second, many forms of training, including desk-top training, need to become more adaptable to workplace conditions. An emerging trend is the move away from conventionally structured courses towards short, self-selected inputs, or electronic performance support that can be fitted into office schedules more readily than longer or pre-scheduled courses. Such formats suit the self-directed learner wishing to tap into essential knowledge on the move, or without leaving their hectic working environment.

Locating learning

Training is only one input to an individual's professional development, and in some cases it may be less significant than their personal observations, experiences and social interactions. If one accepts the view that working and learning are closely linked, the question of where to situate learning does not arise: obviously they will be co-located in space and time. One consequence is that informal learning in the workplace, or wherever it takes place, must suffer from all the same distractions as desk-top training. So have we got anywhere?

Although distractions can be annoying, they are a product of normal working practice, evidence of the organisation's fundamental need to communicate in order to function. As such, they represent real opportunities for dialogue, discovery and learning among employees. Ironically, this fact may have been overlooked by computer- and web-based training advocates, who view distractions as a problem; the sometimes fragile informal learning culture that they signal would suffer greatly if they were to disappear.

That is not to say that all learning occurs informally wherever the employee is working. Just as with desk-top training, quiet areas set aside for study, reflection and analysis provide a vital adjunct to informal learning. Similarly, external training events play an important role in allowing the learner to make sense of their experiences as well as to acquire new knowledge and skills.

Socially conscious design

So far, discussion has focused on the *location* of learning rather than on aspects of the physical environment itself, yet the latter can have a profound psychological effect on employees, with impacts on motivation, job satisfaction and learning. Typical office arrangements range from private workspaces, through to shared or partitioned workspaces and open plan designs, usually allocated according to employee rank. Research in a small US organisation by Rita Gorawara-Bhat (2000) found that intrinsic sources of motivation were more likely to drive workers occupying private workspaces, whereas employees in open workspaces were more sensitive to extrinsic factors (eg pay-and-reward). This may have nothing to do with physical space: it may

> **'By arranging space in ways that foster a sense of physical connectedness, socially-conscious building design can create fertile conditions for informal learning and team development.'**

follow simply from employee status, function and general level of esteem. Yet the personal control offered by private workspaces – over privacy, noise, social interaction and personalisation – can produce significant positive motivation.

Gorawara-Bhat tried to unravel the factors linking physical space to worker satisfaction through an extensive series of interviews inside the organisation. She concluded that, whereas job satisfaction was directly related to employee rank, satisfaction with physical space followed a less straightforward path. In particular, shared and partitioned workspaces appeared to be less satisfying than open plan designs, while private workspaces were still the most satisfying. Gorawara-Bhat did provide the following warning about interpretation, however:

…workspace type cannot be linked to satisfaction with work in a vacuum; therefore, it is important to understand that relationship as situated within the organizational context, both formal and informal. Along these lines, it is less useful to examine which specific attributes of workspace are linked to satisfaction and more relevant to…focus on the totality of the work setting. (Gorawara-Bhat 2000: 130.)

There is no doubt that the nature of the physical setting has a significant effect on learning in organisations. Factors such as privacy, quiet, temperature and related ambient and aesthetic issues clearly affect the degree to which an individual can concentrate on learning activities. Yet the most profound influences of physical space on learning may be more subtle. One's sense of centrality to the core of the organisation, for example, can impact on esteem (and hence eagerness to learn); and, most crucially, the degree to which the space affords social contact among

employees. By arranging space in ways that foster a sense of physical connectedness, socially-conscious building design can create fertile conditions for informal learning and team development. And the office is just one environment where such principles might be deployed. In the 'blur' economy described by Stan Davies and Christopher Meyer (1998), home, office and travelling life are becoming confused. As Gorawara-Bhat puts it:

Beyond the trends of adding more comforts to the workplace and creating environments that foster community and teamwork, the trends have moved to make such environments instantaneously available to busy, travelling workers for whom the boundaries between work and home are becoming ever fuzzier…Such a posture is based in the recognition that creativity does not only happen in the office workspace. (Gorawara-Bhat 2000: 19.)

Learning styles
Overview

There is considerable agreement amongst researchers and practitioners that learners have different characteristic strengths and preferences in the ways they take in and process information. Some learners tend to focus on facts, data, and algorithms; others are more comfortable with theories and mathematical models. Some respond strongly to visual forms of information like diagrams and schematics; others learn better from verbal forms – written and spoken explanations. Some prefer to learn actively and interactively; others function more introspectively and individually. These differences are usually referred to as learning styles.

Polar opposites are often used to define aspects of a learning style: for example, holist versus analyst. Holists like to get an overview of what is to be learned before they are presented with details. Analysts like to look at the details and consider the whole, bit by bit. These opposites are inevitably extreme positions and the majority of learners operate somewhere in the middle, moving slightly in one direction or the other depending on the context.

Adey *et al* (1999) are keen to distinguish learning styles from other terms used in a similar context. They provide the following definitions:

*A **Learning Style** is a deep-rooted preference an individual has for a particular type of learning. One can think of this as being similar to the way one folds one's arms. Each person has a preferred way to do it even though they are quite capable of folding their arms the other way. However, in order to fold one's arms 'the wrong way' one has to think much harder about what one is doing, and it never feels quite as 'natural'…*

*At the other extreme, **Learning Skills** are almost like 'tricks' which are specific, designed to do one job and can be taught. One example of a learning skill is the use of a mnemonic to help remember a series of facts, such as 'Richard Of York Gave Battle In Vain' in order to remember that the seven colours of the rainbow are red, orange, yellow, green, blue, indigo and violet…*

*Somewhere in between these two extremes, the term **Learning Strategy** is used for groups of skills which a learner uses together for a particular purpose. Examples include setting objectives, selecting and formulating questions, and comparing characteristics. (Adey et al 1999: 5.)*

Classification systems

Many researchers have produced classification systems, but five or six are commonly used, and there are many similarities amongst the various systems. In fact, because of the variety of approaches (see Table 7), researchers have begun to group the various systems according to whether they focus on instructional preferences, social interaction models, information-processing models or personality models (see for example O'Connor 1997).

How do these classifications help to improve learning strategies? A good example is the Myers-Briggs Type Indicator® (MBTI) which has been used with thousands of engineering students in the US to examine the effects of psychological differences on career development. The MBTI has also been used as a diagnostic tool for students with learning difficulties and as a focus for negotiating remedial approaches to study. Richard M. Felder of North Carolina State University describes one student categorised as ISTJ (introvert, sensor, thinker and judger) who was failing an electrical circuit course because he was relying too heavily on memorisation and drill (traits of ISTJs). Felder persuaded his student to add strategies based more on a fundamental understanding of the concepts (Felder 1996).

Here he describes one way in which he has applied his Felder-Silverman learning styles model to course design:

I taught five sequential chemical engineering courses in a way that would appeal to a range of learning styles. I presented course material inductively, moving from facts and familiar phenomena to theories and mathematical models rather than always using the 'fundamentals, then applications' approach. I used realistic examples of engineering processes to illustrate basic principles and occasionally provided opportunities for laboratory and plant visits. I stressed active learning experiences in class, reducing the time I spent lecturing. In homework assignments I routinely augmented traditional formula substitution problems with open-ended questions and problem formulation exercises. I used extensive cooperative learning, and tried to get the students to teach one another rather than rely on me exclusively. (Felder 1996.)

An obvious conclusion from this example is that variation in teaching strategy, and opportunities for learners to take an active role in the learning process, are likely to produce successful outcomes for more learners than rigid, one-dimensional approaches.

Using learning styles

Since the 1990s, researchers have come to understand that learners are not fixed forever into one category. How the learner responds to learning opportunities depends on the context and also on the learner's goals. For example, if the course is overloaded with content, learners tend to adopt surface learning tactics; similarly, depending on whether they are preparing for an examination,

Table 7 | Learning style classification systems

Classification	Description
Myers-Briggs Type Indicator®	This model classifies learners according to their preferences on scales derived from psychologist Carl Jung's theory of psychological types: extraverts or introverts; sensors or intuitors; thinkers or feelers; judgers or perceivers. For more detailed information see: http://www.aptcentral.org/aptmbtiw.htm www.gsu.edu/~dschjb/wwwmbti.html members.tripod.com/~PersonalityInstitute/Myers-BriggsTypeIndicator.htm
Felder-Silverman Learning Model	This classification has five categories – sensing or intuitive learners; visual or verbal learners; inductive or deductive learners; active or reflective learners; sequential or global learners. For more detailed information see: http://www.universaleducator.com/LearnStyle/felder.html www2.ncsu.edu/unity/lockers/users/f/felder/public/ILSpage.html
Herrmann Brain Dominance Instrument	This method classifies learners in terms of their relative preferences for thinking in four different modes – left brain cerebral (logical thinkers); left brain limbic (sequential thinkers); right brain limbic (emotional thinkers); right brain cerebral (holistic thinkers). For more detailed information see: http://www.universaleducator.com/LearnStyle/brain.html
Kolb's Learning Style Inventory	This classifies learners as having a preference for (a) concrete experience or abstract conceptualisation, or (b) active experimentation or reflective observation. For more detailed information see: http://www.universaleducator.com/LearnStyle/kolb.html
Honey and Mumford's Classification	Developed from the Kolb's inventory and learning cycle this model has four components – activists; reflectors; pragmatists; theorists. For more detailed information see: http://www.peterhoney.com

using the information on the job, or just trying to understand the subject, tactics will vary (Laurillard 1993). Practitioners have also shown that to function effectively in a professional capacity, workers need to be able to work well in all the learning modes. Information comes in many forms, and much of it will be lost to someone who cannot function well with, for example, both visual and verbal information. An objective of many courses, therefore, is to help learners to build their skills in both their preferred and less preferred modes of learning. This is accomplished by designing courses that 'teach around the cycle', that is, that ensure that materials and processes are presented in multiple modes. Using the Kolb learning cycle, for example, opportunities would be provided:

◘ for the concrete experiencer – laboratories, field work, observations or trigger films

◘ for the reflective observer – logs, journals or brainstorming

◘ for the abstract conceptualiser – lectures, papers and analogies

◘ for the active experimenter – simulations, case studies and homework.

Many researchers conclude that it matters little which learning style model is used: the value comes when learning opportunities are provided across all elements of the model (see for example Felder 1996). Research evidence shows the following benefits are derived from such an approach:

◘ Learners gain insight into their preferred learning styles and formulate successful learning strategies for other styles.

◘ Instructors have a context in which to relate learners' questions, comments and answers.

◘ Optimum problem-solving teams can be formed using people with strengths in each classification.

In short, there are risks associated with placing complex people into simplistic boxes. Practising the full spectrum of learning styles not only improves learning outcomes, but also increases learner satisfaction and self-confidence. As Torrance and Rockenstein (1988) put it:

A learning style may become a learning disability if cultivated at the expense of other ways of learning. (Torrance and Rockenstein 1988: 278.)

Conclusion

While learning theories can inform the design of training and development methods, they should not be interpreted as prescriptions; nor can the selection of one theory or another guarantee training results. In between theory and practice lies a grey area imbued with the culture of the organisation and the collective dispositions of its employees. Depending on how well this grey area is managed – and there are parts of it that are extremely difficult or impossible to manage – a climate of learning will or will not follow. This chapter has explored three factors that fall within this grey area: organisational context, motivation and learning styles. Training and development practitioners need to understand how these factors influence learning, since the impacts may be positive or negative.

Not surprisingly, context – in particular, organisational context – has an important influence on learning. A culture of learning, manifested in time, space and recognition of the value of learning to innovation and organisational development, is a necessary precondition of the learning organisation from which systemic change can follow. Employee attitudes to learning are also crucial. Positive motivation can lead to self-driven, self-directed efforts to solve problems, master new skills and contribute ideas to colleagues, teams and communities; negative motivation can restrict the flow of knowledge and lead to stagnation. Subtle facilitation, combined with appropriate resources and management reinforcement, can sustain the motivation to learn; they can also contribute to a climate of achievement within the organisation from which motivation is a natural outcome. However, motivation will always vary widely among different individuals, and at different times in their careers, as their adaptability and need for growth changes.

Learning style classifications highlight the multiplicity of learning strategies employed by different people, and within the same person in different circumstances. As such, they enrich our understanding about the individuality of learning experiences, and can be helpful in assessing the degree to which training and development methods reflect known variability. In a world clamouring for shorter, faster, more personalised learning activities, the classifications could be used as a means of differentiating learning experiences according to learner preferences. This temptation should be resisted: evidence suggests that learners benefit most from exposure to a full range of learning styles.

So far, this report has explored learning from social, psychological and managerial perspectives, concentrating on the mechanisms by which people acquire knowledge, adapt behaviour and sustain the motivation to learn. The next chapter examines the potential of technology to support and enhance learning processes. It explores what is actually new in e-learning, and questions whether the 'e' should really stand for 'enhanced' rather than 'electronic'.

Endnotes

1 Rogers was critical of conventional instruction, referring to it as 'learning from the neck up'.

2 As distinct from pedagogy, the art and science of teaching children, which Knowles did not believe could be applied to the teaching of adults.

3 Shorter time limits have also been shown to result in faster work.

4 Initial set-up costs for e-learning can be high, however.

4 | How different is e-learning?

Technology...the knack of so arranging the world that we need not experience it.

Max Frisch, 1911–1991

◘ **Although e-learning builds on over 150 years of practice of distance education, it differs markedly from previous technological innovations and does not yet have an established research base.**

◘ **So far e-learning has not produced a new theory of learning; in its present form it can be analysed and interpreted using existing theoretical models.**

◘ **E-learning has, however, defined a new paradigm for learning; a way of working, studying and problem-solving that reflects the growing connectivity of people and learning resources.**

The advent of e-learning has led to many forecasts about massive uptake, and wild predictions about its revolutionary impact on learning in the workplace. A look back at the history of correspondence and distance education is a useful antidote to this kind of ephemera. E-learning has not sprung from a vacuum; it is an evolutionary rather than revolutionary progression from a method of learning that has been slowly gaining acceptance for over 100 years.

The history of learning at a distance begins with the book which, for the first time, enabled scholars to study separately from their teachers. The teaching process itself remained a face-to-face activity until around 150 years ago, however, when developments in transportation and communication technologies associated with the industrial revolution generated interest in distance techniques. Teaching at a distance is, by definition, characterised by the separation of teacher and learner and, in many cases, by a further separation of the learner from the learning group. The interpersonal face-to-face communication of conventional education and training is replaced by a personal mode of communication mediated by technology (Keegan 1996). The early technology was print, and the communication system was postal correspondence between the tutor and the individual learner. This form of education has been labelled 'first generation' distance learning (Nipper 1989).

By the 1970s audio cassettes and broadcast media supplemented printed instruction and added an immediacy in the form of the instructor's voice or moving image, albeit in a one-to-many format. Satellite transmission later joined land broadcast as an alternative approach to delivery. Both methods vastly increased the numbers of learners who could access education, and this 'second generation' has been labelled the 'industrialised phase' of distance learning.

In parallel with developments in distance learning, the results of Skinner's pioneering research on programmed instruction and 'teaching machines' was finding its way into teaching applications and, by the late 1980s, computer-based training (CBT) delivered via magnetic disk and CD-ROM technology had entered into widespread use (see Chapter 2: Learning as behaviour). Arguably, modern forms of web-based training – especially those demonstrating artful instructional design – can be traced back more linearly to programmed learning and CBT than to parallel developments in distance learning.

Communications technology is the hallmark of 'third generation' distance learning, causing Nipper to evaluate the earlier generations as follows:

The main objectives of the first and second generation systems have been the production and distribution of teaching/learning material to the learners. Communication with the learners has been marginal, and communication amongst the learners has been more or less non-existent. (Nipper 1989: 63.)

E-learning belongs to the third generation of distance learning, which has evolved from a one-to-many distribution system to a connected environment where communication is the defining characteristic. Connectivity (or at least the potential for connectivity) also differentiates e-learning from earlier forms of CBT.

Despite its evolutionary status, the e-learning phenomenon has developed very rapidly over the past 10 years as new technologies have appeared in quick succession and have been adopted on a global scale. As a result, the e-learning research base is very thin; furthermore, new areas tend to be investigated before old ones are fully understood. Much of what claims to be research, especially in the training sector, is based on little more than a few questionnaire surveys and the opinions of practitioners. In the analysis that follows, distinctions will be made between

established research findings and areas where there is little to rely on but surveys and opinions. This overview begins with a discussion of the various elements that constitute e-learning.

What is meant by e-learning?
Overview

A review of the e-learning literature reveals considerable ambiguity and often contradictory conceptions about what e-learning actually is. This is particularly true in the training and workplace use of the term. Some definitions of e-learning carry strong overtones of computer-based training transferred to the Internet. The emphasis is on the electronic nature of the content, not the communicative potential of the Web. The UK's Chartered Institute of Personnel and Development takes a different view, however, emphasising the importance of connectivity over stand-alone approaches such as CD-ROMs, satellite broadcasts, video and audio cassettes:

Learning that is delivered, enabled or mediated by electronic technology, for the explicit purpose of training in organisations. It does not include stand-alone technology-based training such as the use of CD-ROMs in isolation. (CIPD 2001.)

In the higher education literature, there is greater consensus that online learning or e-learning means electronic access and interaction with learning materials, fellow learners and tutors. The focus here is on the communicative potential of e-learning, rather than content delivery.

How do these conceptions of e-learning relate to the learning theories discussed in this report? Practitioners of e-learning who emphasise the communicative nature of e-learning draw on constructivist and social practice theories of

> **'To date the primary application of e-learning has been the delivery of structured programmes of study, or courses.'**

learning, often overtly aiming to transform the role of the instructor to that of a facilitator of knowledge construction, and to create a social environment in which learners learn from each other online. Practitioners who emphasise the content delivery side of e-learning often have a behaviourist or cognitive conception of learning, whether consciously or not. They focus on the development of clearly presented content, facilities for testing the learner and multimedia materials for increasing learner motivation. Access to training, reduced costs and speed and retention of learning are the attractions of e-learning for them.

To date the primary application of e-learning has been the delivery of structured programmes of study, or courses. While other approaches to learning do flourish in some organisations (such as those described in Chapter 1: New approaches to learning), the formal course leading to an award or qualification is still dominant. Within the 'course' model, however, approaches vary significantly.

Web-based training

In corporate training, technology is used primarily to deliver content to the end user without significant interaction with (or support from) tutors, peers or managers. A significant industry has grown up around this form of e-learning, spanning content authoring, content asset management, instructional design and learning management. Key objectives of this form of e-learning are *throughput and efficiency* of development, management and delivery of content to learners.

A cursory survey of 30 courses at 16 US companies identified three factors that contribute to the take-up of this form of e-learning in the workplace (ASTD and The MASIE Center 2001):

- Marketing: face-to-face and e-mail promotion, internal champions, testimonials.

- Support: time to take the course in work hours, linking the content to business objectives, status and importance accorded to completing the course, help in transferring the learning to the workplace.

- Incentives: intrinsic motivations contributing to personal development are more powerful than extrinsic factors.

Supported online learning

In higher education, most of the content of the course may be delivered through lectures or through distance-education textual material, but the course is categorised as e-learning because interaction with the tutor, dialogue with other students, the searching for resource materials, conduct of collaborative activities, access to course outlines and supporting material, are all conducted online.

A recent review of 100 research papers about e-learning in higher education identified four major features of good practice (Coomey and Stephenson 2001):

- Dialogue: using e-mail, bulletin boards, 'real-time' chat, asynchronous chat, group discussions and debate, the tutor or moderator structures interactive opportunities into the content of the course.

- Involvement: includes responses in structured tasks, active engagement with material, collaboration and small group activities.

◘ Support: includes periodic face-to-face contact, online tutorial supervision, peer support, advice from experts, feedback on performance, support services and software tools. This is the most important feature of successful online courses, as reported in nearly all of the 100 papers surveyed.

◘ Control: refers to the extent to which learners have control of key learning activities and are encouraged to exercise that control. Responses to exercises, pace and timing, choice of content, management of learning activities, navigation through course content, overall direction and assessment of performance.

Informal e-learning

Beyond these 'course-based' approaches to e-learning are the growing opportunities for technology to support *informal* learning in the workplace. Informal learning is intimately related to job performance; it may not be formally organised into a programme or curriculum by the employer, but it accounts for a good deal of the learning arising out of interactions between colleagues, *ad hoc* personal studies, and the experience of work itself.

The technologies of most relevance to informal e-learning may be grouped into two clusters: information retrieval and knowledge construction. The former covers all forms of search and retrieval software, including databases, data mining applications, information services, electronic performance support and, of course, the Web. The latter covers all forms of communications technology from simple e-mail to virtual whiteboards. Focused on the processes of human dialogue and exchange, they serve to extend the learning opportunity, as follows:

◘ Through web pages and text, audio or video conferencing, the range of people to interact with can transcend physical and functional boundaries.

◘ Through online discussions, there is an opportunity to reflect on and reconceptualise knowledge in its expression to others.

◘ Through online interactions, tacit knowledge is exchanged across a wider spectrum than amongst those who are physically co-located.

◘ The technologies keep a record of interactions, files and web materials that can be retained for later use by those directly involved, and others.

An e-learning typology

This summary of three applications of e-learning demonstrates, therefore, that the scope of the term 'e-learning' extends across a wide range of pedagogies and learning theories. The key characteristics of the three applications are summarised in Table 8.

These distinctions help to clarify apparently contradictory findings in the research literature, for example, over learner engagement with online material, with indicators of success and uptake of online learning, with drop-out rates and evidence of cost savings. In some cases the findings are based on the web-based training model and in others the findings come from a version of supported online learning. Much of the visionary literature draws on the e-community concept, while much of the negative doomsday writing has the CBT-on-the-web concept of e-learning in mind. All are commonly referred to as e-learning, yet they are very different kinds of learning experiences and serve different markets and purposes. Although these three concepts of e-learning represent relatively distinct examples of current practice, in this emerging and fast-changing field there are bound to be other models that overlap and combine aspects of these three.

Implicit in the typology are different underlying expectations of technology – differences that will diminish as corporate trainers, especially, increase their awareness of the value of peer-to-peer and peer-to-tutor interaction in learning. Commentators such as Deborah Schreiber, however, argue that awareness-raising may not be sufficient, and foresee the need for a more radical reappraisal of e-learning strategy:

...many companies procure new [e-learning] technology but often see limited return because they do not know how best to employ it...Designing and implementing distance training that contributes strategically to the organization requires not only a new organizational chart but often a transformation of the corporate culture itself. (Schreiber 1998: 393.)

Is e-learning a new paradigm?

How different, then, is e-learning? Does it represent a new paradigm, or will it pass into obscurity along with educational television, learning machines, overhead projectors and other media which, in their day, were hyped as revolutionary for learning?

There is a long tradition of research into educational technologies that compares learning through 'conventional' means with learning through technology. The outcomes of these studies have been collected together by TeleEducation New Brunswick (2001) under the title 'no significant difference'. In summary, the conclusion is that technologies rarely affect the learning outcomes – when measured by standard end-of-course examinations. While these results apply to e-learning, what the studies fail to account for is the new paradigm that technology, particularly communication technology, has engendered in society at large, and hence in learning as well.

A large part of the so-called new learning paradigm involves a shift from what has been characterized as an atomistic perspective to a more holistic perspective (Spector and Anderson 2000). The atomistic perspective emphasizes individual units of learning (specific and discrete conditions, methods, and outcomes) and tends to treat learners in a similarly isolated manner (focusing

Table 8 | Applications of e-learning

Web-based training	Support online learning	Informal e-learning
Content-focused	Learner-focused	Group-focused
Delivery-driven	Activity-driven	Practice-driven
Individual learning	Small-group learning	Organisational learning
Minimal interaction with tutor	Significant interaction with tutor	Participants act as learners and tutors
No collaboration with other learners	Considerable interaction with other learners	Multi-way interactions among participants

> '...e-learning may not require new theories of learning to account for the nature of the learning experience, but many researchers...conclude that it *is* defining a new learning paradigm.'

assessment on individual learners and evaluation on aggregates of individual assessments). The atomistic perspective can be contrasted with the integrated or holistic perspective, which views a person as a member of a society and as a member of various language communities and communities of practice...This social perspective, and the realization that learning is most often aimed at integrated collections of human activities comprise a holistic perspective of learning. From the holistic perspective, learning is ultimately aimed at improving the understanding of various phenomena and situations and not merely about recalling specific facts or solving specific problems. (Spector 2001: xv–xvi.)

One way of looking at the benefits of e-learning is to disaggregate the pedagogy, the technology and the social dimensions of e-learning. The technology component is the most volatile element of the three. Already we see considerable convergence on to the Web: stand-alone CD-ROMs, video- and tele-conferencing – all have web counterparts or integration mechanisms. The Web itself will evolve beyond recognition, with higher bandwidth, smaller 'screens', mobile access, multimedia communication, and further. The pedagogy element is somewhat more complex. In many ways there is 'nothing new under the sun' regarding learning; there are just fashions and recycling in clothing, ideas, approaches and understandings about how to teach. It has been argued that tutoring online is not a new paradigm; there are skills and tips and good practice but, fundamentally, a good teacher is a good teacher in any medium (Mason 1991).

However, just as grandmother's clothes never quite come back into fashion, educational ideas are also helix-like: when they circle back around, they are subtly different – recognisable but differently

combined or formulated. So it is with e-learning. The components of e-learning could be defined as:

1   multi-way communication amongst learners and between learners and experts

2   hypertextual rather than linear presentation of material

3   integrated access to resources both inside and outside the learning package

4   multimedia forms of interaction and presentation of material.

While these elements may have been available individually before, the combination is new. Furthermore, connectivity over distance and time has had a profound effect not just in terms of learning opportunities, but in a wider social context. Communication through mobile phones has contributed to these changes, but the result is a different expectation about communication and access to information and people. To summarise, e-learning may not require new theories of learning to account for the nature of the learning experience, but many researchers (such as Harasim *et al* 1995, Koschmann 1996, and Spector and Anderson 2000) conclude that it *is* defining a new learning paradigm:

Profound changes at all levels of society and technology demand new educational responses. The paradigm for education in the twenty-first century that is emerging is network learning. Based on global interactivity, collaborative learning, and lifelong access to educational activities and resources, it provides an approach that emphasizes international connectivities and engenders new ways of working, studying and problem solving. (Harasim et al 1995: 278.)

What are the benefits and limitations of e-learning?
Overview

Interactivity with course content, and particularly with fellow learners and tutors, is increasingly seen to be the most significant element of e-learning. Evidence of its value in higher education is exemplified by the comments of a student on a supported online Masters programme offered by the Open University:

The opportunity for student–student collaboration has to be, for me, the most stimulating part of the programme and the greatest opportunity in developing online learning. (IET 2000.)

The results of studies of individual e-learning programmes have shown that support and feedback are the most highly valued aspects of the provision, and contribute directly to successful uptake and completion (ASTD and The MASIE Center 2001). It would be hard to find research evidence that interactivity – whether with people or with learning materials – was unnecessary or undesirable. On this basis, far from a diminished role for teachers in technology-enabled learning environments, Spector foresees an increased function:

In the 1990s it was suggested that distributed learning and tele-collaboration would make traditional classroom teachers obsolete (see for example, Koschmann, 1996). This has not happened. What has happened is that learners, teachers, designers and researchers have realized that collaboration at a distance is often quite difficult and challenging. The role of the teacher is not likely to be eliminated by technology, although technology will surely affect the roles of both teachers and learners. The role of teaching in

technology-intensive settings is more difficult and more crucial than ever before. (Spector 2001: xiv.)

Research does show that interactivity is costly, however; costly in terms of running training events, but also in terms of time, both of the tutor or facilitator and the learner. In practice, then, it is reasonable to ask, 'If some is good, is more better?' Here there is evidence that more interaction can lead to overload, unread messages and inefficiency – even when the interaction has been carefully structured and managed (Mason 1999). Referring back to theories of learning, it is obvious why this is so. Learning consists of a number of elements and stages, of which interactivity is only one. Designing a learning programme or event is about balancing all the elements for the particular learners and the context in which the learning takes place.

Researchers and practitioners of e-learning have drawn up lists of the advantages of the new medium, as exemplified in Box 2. Such lists are inevitably 'context independent' and, in practice, it is often noted how these advantages are simultaneously disadvantages as well. For example, the flexibility of the medium easily leads learners to allow other priorities to come before logging on to the course or group work. The much vaunted interactivity easily leads to overload. The ability to jump from one resource to the next on the Web (ie hypertext) can be overused so that relatedness becomes an end in itself, and meaning is lost.

Box 2: Positive features of e-learning

Stephenson (2001) points to the following advantages of e-learning:

- Easy access to and interrogation of high volumes of diverse learning resources, including texts, pictures, library materials, learning tools and other aids to learning selected by the instructor.
- Ease of access to other materials from other sources, including non-educational sources.
- Ease of access to experts, inside and external to the institution.
- Interaction in various modes: teacher–student, student–student, student–learning materials.
- Interaction in various time dimensions: in real time (synchronous) or over a period (asynchronous).
- Access to a range of personal support: by e-mail with tutor and mentors, or through peer group discussions.
- Ease of navigation to sources and persons within and outside the training course or materials.
- Logging or tracking of activities for personal records, sharing or assessment.
- Multiple levels of engagement to different depths of understanding, different volumes of data, difficulty of learning activities, according to individual capacity or interest.
- Feedback loops, either from teachers, peers and others, or from within the materials themselves through progress checking, quizzes and online assessment.
- Linkages to other media, such as sound, video and TV.
- Ease of access to simulations of dangerous or complex activities for learning purposes.
- Choice of learning styles within the same package according to the needs of the learner.
- Global connectivity and collaboration opportunities.
- Flexibility of access from different locations.

Usability in web-based training

A usability study of three e-learning products was carried out to understand 'why people can't use e-learning' (Quinn 2001). The results identified four serious problems common to these and many e-learning courses:

- counter-intuitive reading order of on-screen material
- failure to relate to the real-world experience of the user
- poor presentation of key information
- lack of accessibility, even in the most basic sense.

Clearly, this research applies to the web-based training model of e-learning rather than the supported online learning or informal e-learning models. Given this, the authors conclude that e-learning companies must adopt a usability strategy during product development. They quote figures of the failure to complete e-learning courses as anywhere between 30 and 75 per cent, and claim that poor usability contributes to learner frustration and negativity about the medium. Another issue they raise is internationalisation: interfaces must be flexible so that they can be adapted to suit the needs of diverse cultures.

A KnowledgeNet (2001) White Paper is also critical of the content-driven approach to e-learning:

While technology-based training offers flexibility, cost-effectiveness, and rapid deployment capability, most experts (and enterprise training managers) agree that technology-based training to date has largely failed as an effective training medium. (KnowledgeNet 2001.)

'There is considerable research demonstrating the value of online peer learning, collaborative small group activities and discussion and debate...'

The report goes on to characterise much of what passes for e-learning in organisations as 'first generation', which has largely failed to harness the full potential of the Internet and new media technologies:

While some providers are dressing up their offerings with online mentoring through store-and-forward methods such as bulletin boards or email, the core training products remain text-based and ineffective. Some vendors also have been experimenting with low-fidelity, streamed audio and video and low-quality, intermittent 'web casts' featuring live instructors. In spite of these early advances, e-learning in its first incarnation lacks effectiveness. (KnowledgeNet 2001.)

The authors call for e-learning experiences to be multimedia, citing the commonly accepted finding that learners retain knowledge much more effectively when all senses are engaged. They also stress the importance of knowledgeable, passionate instructors who have adapted their communicative skills to synchronous or asynchronous interaction online. Finally, they recommend the customisation of the learning environment to the individual learner's needs, speed and timetable.

Collaboration in supported online learning

Turning to the supported online learning model, in which the focus is on the communicative and collaborative opportunities of e-learning, the evidence is less critical, but still mixed. There is considerable research demonstrating the value of online peer learning, collaborative small group activities and discussion and debate, although much of the evidence comes from areas of the curriculum that lend themselves to reflection, tacit understanding and diffuse knowledge domains.

However, there are research studies that identify the problems and dissatisfactions with e-learning in the supported model. Three drawbacks are inevitably highlighted (Mason and Weller 2000).

1 The time-consuming nature of online collaboration and discussion, both for the learner and for the tutor/moderator/instructor.

2 The resistance of many students long practised in individual study, to undertake collaborative activities, especially those involving team assessment.

3 The need for experience and understanding of the dynamics of online interaction on the part of the course designers and tutors in order to structure an online environment that encourages students to interact regularly and positively throughout the course.

An emerging role for informal e-learning

Research addressing the benefits and limitations of informal e-learning is very scarce. The Education Development Center in Massachusetts has conducted substantial research on informal learning in manufacturing companies, and claims that 70 per cent of job-related learning takes place outside formal training events. However, this study is not specifically focused on electronic forms of informal learning (Stamps 1998; Dobbs 2000).

A CIPD (Stern and Sommerlad 1999) study examining workplace learning, culture and performance concludes that the visionary view of new technology and global competitiveness driving a new demand for informal kinds of learning in the workplace is difficult to substantiate with hard evidence. In fact, the study claims that most broad-brush surveys of employers' training practices are concerned with training that is pedagogically structured. Workplace learning based on experiential modes of learning and integrated into production processes and the way work is organised, is difficult to define, capture and record, especially with survey instruments. The study accepts:

We are mostly in the dark about the nature and extent of this kind of non-formal or informal learning. (Stern and Sommerlad 1999: 3.)

However, the lack of data on informal e-learning should not be interpreted as lack of activity. In fact, almost every aspect of working and learning is being affected by 'network technologies', as Spector (2001) succinctly describes:

One change due to network technologies involves the blurring of the traditional distinction between learning and working. Individuals may shift seamlessly from performing a work activity into a system-initiated help environment. Workers may put one complex task on hold while taking time out for a focused tutorial. Individuals may initiate background agents to gather information on selected topics which are then pushed into windows that appear in the user's desktop work environment. Workers may shift from working alone on one isolated task to seeking guidance and advice from a networked community involved in similar activities. (Spector 2001: xvi.)

A recent research paper by Gerhard Fischer and Eric Scharff (1998) on technologies for self-directed learning makes the following claim:

One of the major misunderstandings in our current debate about enhancing learning with new media is the assumption that technological advances will, by virtue of their very existence, improve the

quality of learning. New technologies and media must be more than add-ons to existing practices. New technologies and learning theories must together serve as catalysts for fundamentally rethinking what learning, working, and collaborating can be and should be in the next century. (Fischer and Scharff 1998: 4.)

A major finding in current business re-engineering efforts is that the use of information technology has a more disappointing return on investment than expected. It is generally accepted that the major reason for this is that information technologies have been used to mechanise old ways of doing business, rather than fundamentally rethinking underlying work processes (Landauer 1995).

These studies of the application of new technologies to workplace learning present a picture not of technology failure, but of human failure to engage with the challenge that technology offers for transformation. In many cases, the theories about how people learn and about how they learn in the workplace have not been applied in the design and support of learning.

Dispelling myths

While the exploitation of e-learning technology has been patchy and even misapplied, there has been no patchiness in the hype about the promise of e-learning. Inevitably myths about e-learning continue to gather momentum through unrelenting mass media coverage. In a recent edition of the online journal, TechKnowLogia, Cher Ping Lim, of Nanyang Technological University in Singapore, questioned four of these myths:

1   E-learning is all about technology:

For decades, educators, administrators and researchers have been lured into the fantasy that radio, television and videotapes are going to take over the human instructor. In 1922, Thomas Edison predicted that motion picture was likely to supplant the use of textbooks. As we now know, such optimistic predictions were shattered by subsequent media comparison studies that failed to prove that any one medium is superior to another…The success of e-learning in a corporation depends on the way e-learning is situated within that environment. If nothing significant changes in that environment save the introduction of e-learning, few, if any, important effects can be expected. (Lim 2001: 1.)

2   E-learning is all about information delivery:

Employees in the 21st century are already bombarded with too much information. With so much information available, corporations need people who can synthesize meaning from large bodies of diverse knowledge…E-learning then, must be about making possible successful knowledge management to leverage upon the intellectual capital of the entire corporation. (Lim 2001: 1.)

3   E-learning is all about replacing existing training with the web:

Much too often, e-learning courses have been attempting to replace traditional learning and teaching media without much thought to their underlying pedagogical principles. For example, from textbooks to e-books, or from overhead slides to PowerPoint slides…Without considering the strengths and weaknesses of each medium, e-learning courses may adversely affect the

learning experiences of course participants. (Lim 2001: 2.)

4   E-learning is all about interactions between computers and learners:

Many e-learning courses have over-emphasized the interactions between the computer and the learner. These interactivities are often seen as control over pace, choice of activities and sequences…E-learning must be about providing the interactions among the employees and their communities to develop the competitive advantage of the corporation. (Lim 2001: 2.)

The author goes so far as to claim that e-learning is a double-edged sword: it can be used either to enhance the corporation's competitive advantages *or* to amplify their disadvantages. It can foster a learning community or cause abstraction and individualism among employees. No direct evidence is given to support these claims, but they do point to the importance of the wider organisational context in e-learning design. Martyn Sloman's 21 propositions about e-learning also endorse this view that the 'Internet changes everything', including training. It gives new meaning to the concept of a learning organisation by facilitating the integration of training with business strategies (Sloman 2001).

Collis and Moonen (2001) dispel the myth that e-learning is about overcoming distance. For them, the key to e-learning is flexibility:

- flexibility in the amount of learning material accessed

- flexibility in time of access to materials

- flexibility in the way the material is presented.

> '...while technology...allows courses to be accessed much more rapidly than before, there is no evidence that e-learning can speed up the process of learning.'

In short, *time* is now the barrier that distance used to be. As Thomas H. Davenport notes:

We live in an attention economy. At this point in history, capital, labor, and information are all in plentiful supply. Computer processing power increases by leaps and bounds, but the processing power of the human brain stays the same. Telecommunications bandwidth is not a problem; human bandwidth is. (Davenport 2001.)

Paradoxically, then, while technology supports much higher levels of communication in the workplace, and allows courses to be accessed much more rapidly than before, there is no evidence that e-learning can speed up the process of learning. Its flexibility simply provides greater control over when, where and how the learning takes place.

A Hambrecht report on e-learning has countered the myth that enthusiasm for e-learning is waning due to the slowing economy and consequent corporate belt-tightening (Urdan and Weggen 2001). Its survey of leading public and private learning management systems' vendors showed no downturn in the sales or predicted sales of these infrastructure products for e-learning:

This speaks to the cost benefits of e-learning as well as its ability to create competitive advantage for companies increasingly dependent on the strength and effective deployment of their 'human capital.' We expect that, given its generally favourable cost structure compared to instructor-led training, the market for learning management platforms will continue to grow dramatically through 2001, even in a more difficult economic climate. (Urdan and Weggen 2001: 2.)

These studies show that while e-learning has spawned many myths and much exaggerated coverage about its transformation potential, there is evidence that the medium remains vibrant and is only in its infancy as far as understanding its true applications.

Conclusion

Any media-related term that is popularised undergoes a similar trajectory: at first it is a buzz word; then it becomes overused so the early-adopters move on to coin new words and concepts, and finally it either dies out completely or finds its rightful place as signifying a particular idea or practice. Already the early adopters of e-learning are looking around for new words or are adapting the term to cover new meanings. M-learning, meaning mobile e-learning 'on the road' or anywhere outside the office, is the latest buzz word. Meanwhile, e-learning is being redefined as 'enhanced' learning or even 'experiential' learning.

These substitutions for 'electronic' reflect a realisation that it is not the electronic nature of e-learning that captures its true value, but rather the opportunity to integrate working, learning and community in the workplace. Furthermore, the earlier e-learning adopters have come full circle in rejecting an 'either-or' view of learning online versus face-to-face. So-called *blended* solutions often offer the most satisfactory outcomes: 50/50 models of face-to-face and online learning can combine the best of both worlds; even 75 per cent online with one face-to-face or residential meeting is successful in overcoming the limitations of online learning, while benefiting from its overall cost-effectiveness and flexibility.

Importantly, blended approaches can encourage
participants to make *better* use of face-to-face
contact in the knowledge that preparations and
follow-up can be conducted online. Totally online
courses should be reserved for those contexts in
which it is impossible or unreasonable for learners
to come together – typically international events
and training courses, or projects in which learners
cannot leave their operational setting.
Synchronous technologies provide a partial
substitute.

What does this mean for the continued investment
in face-to-face and residential facilities of fixed
location training? On the one hand, blended
solutions to learning have strong pedagogical
justifications: exposure to ideas through several
different media definitely improves understanding
and take-up (Collis and Moonen 2001). On the
other hand, the provision of multiple media is
more costly. The Open University has found that
students are very positive about electronic tuition,
but are less happy when it is a complete substitute
for face-to-face tutorials. This has left the
institution with all the costs of managing physical
and technology-based support.

As students adjust to the notion and to the
practicalities of learning online, and as the number
of students with home access to the Internet
grows, these replication costs may be the
inevitable price of change and innovation. With
each passing year, more and more administrative
and tutorial services are being offered online, with
greater and greater value evident in the
investment in online infrastructure. However, in
higher education, just as in the workplace, there
are areas of the curriculum, types of experiences,
and forms of tacit knowledge that for the
foreseeable future still require face-to-face
interaction to understand.

5 | Closing perspectives

There is nothing so practical as a good theory.

Kurt Lewin, 1890–1947

◘ **As an approach to workplace learning, instruction, by itself, is inadequate to 'deliver' learning in the new competitive environment. Greater experimentation with alternative and richer mixes of learning processes is needed, in particular blends of self-directed, experiential and socially mediated learning.**

◘ **Informal learning through work, through teams and through other forms of social co-operation has been seriously underestimated. The value of *working* together is well recognised; we now need to recognise the value of *learning* together in physical, virtual or mixed communities.**

◘ **The idea that e-learning would deliver efficiency gains, simply by replacing face-to-face training with technology, has largely been discredited. Its value in providing flexibility is clear, but the new challenge is to capitalise on its support for interactivity.**

Under pressure to achieve at work, many training and development practitioners could be forgiven for dealing with their immediate priorities rather than allotting time to the study of learning theories. Yet we know that good theories can have enormous practical value. So what is this value in the case of learning theories, and what can the theories tell us about where the next wave of innovation might occur?

The most convincing group to answer these and other questions emerging from this report is the practitioners themselves – those who are living and breathing corporate learning. Consequently, a group of leading HRD professionals[1] was invited to

assess the significance of the report and offer their vision of the challenges ahead; in short to shift the debate from theory into practice by giving a voice to those responsible for bringing innovation to the field.

This chapter attempts to weave the practitioners' comments into a narrative conclusion for the report. The intention is to surround the report's key messages with a commentary that is identifiable and meaningful to practitioners. The chapter closes by profiling a number of aspects of workplace learning that are inadequately understood at present, but which may have a significant impact on future practice.

Comments and conclusion

The most significant conclusion arising from this review of learning theories is that none of the approaches presented in Chapter 2 *by itself* offers an adequate solution to the 'delivery' of learning in the new competitive environment. This is perhaps most noticeable in the case of the behaviourist approach which, through its focus on instruction, deals inadequately with the social and experiential dimensions of learning. It is also true of the cognitive approach, which relies too heavily on the acquisition of knowledge, rather than the development of practical capabilities.

In stressing the inseparability of learning from activity, the constructivist approach holds much promise for organisations. But it is demanding on the learner and can be difficult and time-consuming to scale. Approaches based on social practice offer organisations a compelling alternative, not least because they operate through many of its existing channels and relate intimately to work objectives. Yet not all organisations have the culture in place to benefit fully from this approach.

While none of the theoretical approaches is adequate by itself, an appropriate *mixture* of approaches could be. The evolution in thinking from *training to learning* is epitomised by the movement towards a richer and evolving palette of learning processes that reflect better the needs of individuals and the demands of work.

Greater experimentation with learning processes is therefore required, in particular ones intended to kindle interest in self-directed learning, or which link learning more directly into routine work activities. Experimentation plays an important role here in deepening the evidence base on which decisions about learning are made: new ideas must flow off the table into practice in order to enable effective comparison.

Comments from HRD professionals

The report has huge potential value and I am interested in using it to prompt a review within elements of my HR development strategy.

The report puts some simple coherence around complex topics, making it very powerful. Its frameworks allow us to hold up our practice against the theory, and to audit for internal consistency.

The report will be most valuable to people involved in the design or management of new training activities, especially those asked to think strategically. I wish I had had access to the report 18 months ago.

Awareness about learning theories in the training and development profession is quite patchy, often limited to a few well-known thinkers – Belbin on teams, Honey and Mumford on learning styles, and Maslow on motivation. As a result, trainers tend to feel their way through projects using their experience and intuition. Although many of the ideas in the report were familiar, bringing them together in this way was very useful.

Boundaries are blurring between knowledge, learning and training, and the report will be helpful in developing ideas and promoting discussion – it contains the right avenues of enquiry.
This report will resonate with people who are thinking about organisational performance, culture and innovation. It helps to see how we can improve. There is a long way to go, but senior practitioners will certainly recognise the issues.

Generally business does not advance on a strong body of theory, but this report will be helpful. It will allow practitioners to ground what they do in theory, and to develop applications for measurement, testing and intervention.

The report has great potential value; it will encourage organisations to review how directly they can manage work-based learning – see what is being learnt, review and assess, question their own effectiveness – thus leading to change and improvement.

The report can't move the debate forward by itself; that depends on people having the patience to read what it says and start experimenting with new forms of learning. But it sets the scene for substantial changes in the profession, and provides an excellent basis for discussion with colleagues.

I did think the report was incredibly theoretical. Therefore my gut reaction is that it is going to be of limited value for practitioners. A short summary of its key ideas is essential.

I did find the report quite theoretical, but that is how it was positioned. Portraits of corporate practice would have been a great help and hopefully these will appear in further reports.

We have a strong theoretical base for understanding learning in the traditional sense, but I think we're making it up as we go along with e-learning. Anything that helps us to understand e-learning is a good thing.
We definitely need more work on e-learning: why people are moving to it; what benefits they are finding. There are not enough useful data out there for practitioners to make decisions.

Many people have trouble distinguishing between learning and training. I find it useful to focus on learning rather than training as my chief goal. Training is one of several methods of securing learning objectives, rather than an end in its own right.

The conventional training course has been successful for so long, partly because it appears to be an efficient way of 'delivering' learning objectives in the short term. Because it yields an immediate response (completed training packages/courses, test results), it gives the impression that learning has occurred. It also seems to lend validity and control to the work of trainers.

In fact, the routine use of instruction in training, as exemplified by the 'tell and listen' presentation, is in danger of becoming a rather conservative approach, particularly when it is delivered poorly or does not connect effectively to the wider organisational context. So prevalent is its use, that many employees have become conditioned to regard training *as* instruction and, furthermore, to regard learning *as* training. The net result is that the employees develop a high expectation that learning happens on training courses that involve presentations and a binder of materials to take away at the end.

Similarly, many trainers and managers adhere, sometimes unconsciously, to the view that learning, training and instruction are one and the same. Even when this distinction is fully understood the alternative, less conservative, models may be seen as more demanding both by the recipients of the training and those responsible for organising it. And they would be right.

An analogy may be drawn with the tendency of some employees to rely too heavily on their job description in order to interpret their work responsibilities. Few people, now, would disagree that this approach can act as a brake on creativity by inhibiting the exploration of job roles and boundaries. Nonetheless, it might be perceived by some as an easy, low-risk strategy for fulfilling the employment contract and, if it was seen in this way by the majority of staff, then managers might also find reason to support it.

People have the feeling that they can only learn when they come on a course. We need to help people understand that it can happen anywhere; that every interaction with a client, supplier or colleague is a potential learning opportunity; that learning is a state of mind.

If I ask one of our employees what they have learned today, I sometimes receive the reply, 'Nothing, I haven't been on a course since last year.' This has always intrigued me, and concerned me, since most of what people learn occurs informally through work. It's just not recognised, even by the learners themselves.

In thinking about how our role might change over the next five years, I think we have to be prepared for a total rethink. It's important that we move away from a narrow focus on training, towards the wider goal of learning. It's only then that we shall be supporting our business genuinely; only then that we shall respond quickly enough to the pace of change.

Senior managers especially should get their heads around the report – people working at board level, drawn from across the organisation, who support the development of others. The report will enhance their understanding, and help to create space for innovation.

As everything else changes – context, technology, content – the one constant is the requirement to learn.

Many training groups brand themselves as learning departments, yet there is a vast, fundamental distinction between learning and the training they deliver.

Not enough theoretical ideas are brought into the planning process. Faced with a request for training, it's easy to ignore new ideas, apply existing formulae, and then wonder why training isn't always effective.

It's essential for training programmes to give employees the space to learn from each other, not just listen to other people's commentaries on what they should do. We're trying to build transferable problem-solving skills, not just transmit knowledge.

Properly designed training courses will continue to have an important role in human resources development. I'd be unhappy, however, if in any one training day more than about an hour was spent listening to experts. If transfer of knowledge is the goal, this can be achieved more effectively through pre-reading or electronic resources.

The days of trainers standing up and lecturing all day, saying 'thank you', and departing are basically over. Most of our training is now built around experiential learning techniques like management games and simulations, case studies, scenarios and problem-solving.

The conventional cycle of planning training, sending people on courses, and assessing what things they have learned is too lengthy to respond to the pace of change experienced by many firms. Other tools than the training course are needed to support employee learning more flexibly and quickly.

This self-sustaining cycle would need to be arrested at some point in order to let other approaches flourish, and so it is with instruction. Learners who demand instruction, and receive it, will be inhibited in their development of self-directed learning.

What are the implications of making greater use of alternative approaches? And what might be the interim steps? Panel members offered a number of suggestions: first of all, there is a need to pause when considering training responses, and to be more inventive, holistic, and to draw on a richer set of learning processes (and hence theories).

Second, there is a need to recognise the value, extent and legitimacy of informal modes of learning – learning through work, through teams and through other forms of social interaction, for example. This area has been seriously underestimated by organisations despite a weight of common-sense evidence that most learning takes place informally. The value of *working* together has been established beyond doubt by years of research on teamworking; we now need to recognise the value of *learning* together in physical, virtual or mixed communities, living off our own wits and resources.

Regarding e-learning, the early adopters' view that it would deliver efficiency gains, simply by replacing face-to-face trainers with technology, has largely been discredited. Its value in providing flexibility is already being taken for granted; flexibility in time, space and design. The new challenge is to capitalise on its support for interactivity between people, inspired by business imperatives and moderated by 'trainers as facilitators.'

Here we run up against the issue of time. Intensive online interaction is time-consuming and it must be seen to deliver value to the participant and to the business. Space is needed in employee schedules to get the best out of the new medium, but it will be necessary to show how online interaction translates into business results.

Many in-house trainers haven't focused on the fact that their role is changing underneath them. The ideas in this report should help to wake them up to this fact.

Learning is no longer a 'nice to have', it is a 'must have'. Learning is part of the manager's role. It is their day job.

The key question is how do we make learning as effective as possible? Trainers are going to have to be humble about this. A lot of what we do tends to be unreflective and, perhaps, ineffective. The profession has not been served well in theoretical terms. We need to experiment now with new approaches and deal with the grey areas in our knowledge.

In amongst the noise we are experiencing a 'new dawn', occasioned by the catalytic effect of e-learning. It is certainly right that we take time to reflect on what we know and ask questions of ourselves.

If there is something we need to look up at work, or even at home, what do we do? The chances are that we log on to the Internet to find out for ourselves. It's these informal learning activities that really make a difference – training courses just wouldn't respond quickly enough.

My frustration is that there isn't enough understanding amongst organisations about how frequently they are learning. Unless they see learning formalised, they don't recognise it as learning. They feel they are learning something only when someone stands up and tells them something.

We talk fondly about developing a learning culture, but you can't do that overnight. When you are expecting people to deliver some pretty stretching business results, they don't see learning as a high priority. They can't make the connection. We're too busy trying to reach the goals to invest in our people.

There is a scepticism about what exactly e-learning is delivering. One of the mistakes people made in first moving to e-learning was thinking it would replace contact time with other learners and with the trainer.

The chief benefit of e-learning is flexibility in place, time and format. But it will be a challenge to get people learning through the web. We'll need to look closely at what will draw them in, keep them there, and how will it help them to learn.

E-learning doesn't so much replace face-to-face learning as supplement and extend it. A good analogy is with e-mail. Nobody in their right mind would replace all their telephone conversations and meetings with e-mail. It's a judgement each time between the various channels: e-mail, telephone or face-to-face.

In our case a web portal now assists a lot of our learning activities, but it's not just a catalogue of courses. We try to provide learners with a rich set of options in terms of the way they learn; some of them will take courses, but others will learn through communities of practice or through contact with professional bodies and universities. Others will simply draw down on critical resources when they need them. We can't predict the situations they will all be in, so giving them flexibility is key.

Panel members were unanimous in endorsing 'blended learning' as the way forward. In the first instance this means combining virtual and face-to-face forms of delivery to provide opportunities for interpretation and discussion of inputs obtained over the Web, and for community formation. As this is adopted, blending informal and formal modes of learning offers a further challenge. We know that learning is a more or less continuous process, whereas training is discrete; clearly some rebalancing is required.

Other forms of blend might also be considered. Individual and collaborative activities can be mixed to help develop social and well as individual learning skills; and opportunities for facilitating learning 'through' work as well as 'at' work may be identified to help ground learning activities in work experience. Rather than focusing on just one element of a learning strategy, e-learning can support all aspects of this richer mix.

The role of e-learning in supporting web-based instruction and content delivery are well known but, other than in a few well-known cases, we are only beginning to understand how technology can support the experiential and social foundations of learning. One thing is clear: training and development practitioners will retain a new and exciting role in this mix; if anything, their role will be expanded.

Finally, the move towards a richer set of learning processes means that learners need a correspondingly stronger sense of motivation. The best way of encouraging this learner-centred directedness lies not only in external rewards or punishments but through helping learners to take small and regular steps towards a sense of achievement. The expectation of success is probably the strongest driver of self-directed learning of all.

Challenging training objectives such as the development of inter-personal skills, leadership and values typically require intensive communication, most likely face-to-face. However, once the group has met it can continue to work effectively online, with regular physical meetings helping to sustain momentum.

The Web is the perfect medium for certain types of learning. It achieves speed and spread like no other medium, but you have to remember that there is a human being at the other end. They have their own ideas about what and how they should learn, which may differ from those of the designer.

The key message is blended learning: combining e-learning with face-to-face sessions. Expecting learning to happen on the desk-top is unrealistic. If left to chance it may not happen.

Two factors strike me as most interesting: the fact that individuals have their own unique styles of learning; and the fact that learning is so dependent on context. 'One size fits all' policies that deliver uniform training experiences overlook this fact in favour of expediency, and risk being ineffective.

Learning about interpersonal skills is manifestly better when working on real problems. This could involve role play, simulations or other experiential methods. The important point is that you are there, participating with warm-blooded people.

A lot of people still want to go on courses. Taking them away and putting the content online could lead to an uproar by staff.

The more trainers and coaches are aware of the learning culture in which they are operating, the context of the particular programme, the learning styles of the participants and their attitudes to change, the more effective their work will be.

We are trying to ensure that learning and development needs are linked explicitly to business outcomes. So we encourage people to articulate their learning needs in terms of outputs and impact for the organisation. We want learning to be business-owned, not an HR responsibility.

Getting people to take responsibility for their own self-development, rather than rely on managers and training professionals to tell them what they need to learn, is a great idea, but difficult to implement. We need to create a culture where people walk into work thinking, 'This is what I am interested in, this is what motivates me, and this is how I will do it.'

Areas for future study

Learning was studied and debated throughout the twentieth century, resulting in a profound body of literature and ideas. There is no sign that interest in the topic is abating – rather the converse. Continuing theoretical developments and the advent of new technologies will keep pushing the fringes of our knowledge. Several areas stand out as deserving urgent and concerted enquiry.

1   The future of the course:

   ◘ Blended learning is the current buzz phrase; indeed the balance between digital and face-to-face learning is a fertile area of study (both are legitimate and complementary). However, a more profound question is how to integrate formal study programmes with informal learning approaches. Technologies can be used to extend and enrich courses or short events to allow more productive and continuous follow-up. In order to achieve this we need to understand more fully how to develop online communities and alumni groups, and how to make web-casts and online events more compelling.

   ◘ The notion of learning objects is also very much in vogue. They promise to restructure our idea of the course by taking a granular, personalised approach to content management and delivery. But how useful in the longer term is the 20-minute learning object? How far can learning be modularised before it is trivialised and ineffective? How can learning objects support socially-mediated learning?

2   The role of the trainer, and of the learner:

   ◘ Convergence, or at least increased complementarity, of training, development and knowledge functions in an organisation is much discussed. Yet this goal will require wholesale re-evaluation of the training function. What new responsibilities should training and development practitioners be seeking to take up, and what areas of their profession need to be unlearned?

   ◘ The employee, too, will need to take on new responsibilities for learning as informal approaches take hold, content is available 'on tap', and self-directed learning is assumed (in short, the skills of 'learning to learn'). What are these new responsibilities, and how can the instinct to learn best be encouraged?

3   The issue of where to situate learning is constantly under consideration. The busy office, in order to link learning to work? The quiet, resource-rich library? The training centre? The home? Out in the field? The era of mobile learning will obviously impact on our conception of where and how people learn. Some will call for learning 'on the fly' in the form of immediate information updates and access to knowledge repositories (for example repair and other service personnel needing access to technical material while on house calls). What impact will miniature screens and keypads have on the presentation of information and the nature of communication? What dangers ensue from blurring the distinction between work and home life?

Endnote

1   A list of this helpful group appears in the acknowledgements.

References

ADEY P., FAIRBROTHER R. W. and WILIAM D. (1999)

Learning Styles and Strategies: A review of research. London, School of Education, King's College London.

ARGYRIS C. (1976)

Increasing Leadership Effectiveness. New York, Wiley.

ARGYRIS C. (1994)

On Organisational Learning. Oxford, Blackwell.

ARGYRIS C. (1998)

'An interview with Chris Argyris'. *Strategy+Business*, first quarter, 1998 – at: http://www.strategy-business.com/press/article/?art=14746&pg=0

ARGYRIS C. and SCHÖN D. A. (1974)

Theory in Practice: Increasing professional effectiveness. San Francisco, Jossey-Bass.

ARGYRIS C. and SCHÖN D. A. (1978)

Organization Learning: A theory of action perspective. Reading, Mass., Addison-Wesley.

ASTD and THE MASIE CENTER (2001)

E-Learning: 'If We Build It, Will They Come?'. American Society of Training Directors/The MASIE Center – at: www.masie.com/masie/research reports/ASTD_Exec_Summ.pdf

BANDURA A. (1977)

Social Learning Theory. Englewood Cliffs, NJ, Prentice Hall.

BANDURA A. (1986)

Social Foundations of Thought and Action: A social cognitive theory. Englewood Cliffs, NJ, Prentice Hall.

BECKER G. S. (1964)

Human Capital: A theoretical and empirical analysis, with special reference to education. Chicago, University of Chicago Press (3rd edition 1993).

BECKER G. S. (2001)

'Talking human capital with Professor Gary S. Becker, Nobel Laureate'. *Learning in the New Economy*, Spring 2001 – at: www.linezine.com

BLACKLER F. (1995)

'Knowledge, knowledge work and organizations: an overview and interpretation'. *Organization Studies*. Vol. 16, No. 16. pp1021–46.

BLACKLER F., CRUMP N. and MCDONALD S. (1999)

'Managing experts and competing through innovation: an activity theoretical analysis'. *Organization*. Vol. 6, No.1. pp5–31.

BLOOM B.S. (ed.) (1956)

Taxonomy of Educational Objectives: The classification of educational goals. Handbook 1: Cognitive domain. London, Longmans, Green and Company.

BOJE D. M. (1991)

'The storytelling organization: a study of story performance in an offices-supply firm'. *Administrative Science Quarterly*. Vol. 36. pp106–26.

BORTON T. (1970)

Reach, Touch and Teach. New York, McGraw-Hill.

BOUD D., KEOGH R. and WALKER D. (eds) (1985)

Reflection: Turning experience into learning. London, Kogan Page.

BOUD D. and FELETTI G. (1997)

The Challenge of Problem-Based Learning. 2nd edition. London, Kogan Page.

BOSHYK Y. (ed.) (2000)

Business Driven Action Learning: Global Best Practices. London, Macmillan Business.

BROWN J. S. and DUGUID P. (1991)

'Organizational learning and communities of practice: toward a unified view of working, learning, and innovation'. *Organization Science*. Vol. 2. pp40–57 (at: www.parc.xerox.com/ops/members/brown/papers/orglearning.html).

CAMPBELL S. F. (1976)

Piaget Sampler: An introduction to Jean Piaget through his own words. New York, John Wiley & Sons.

CIPD (2001)

Training and Development 2001: Survey report. London, Chartered Institute of Personnel and Development.

COLLIS B. and MOONEN J. (2001)

Flexible Learning in a Digital World. London, Kogan Page.

COLLISON C. and PARCELL G. (2001)

Learning to Fly: Practical lessons from one of the world's leading knowledge companies. Oxford, Capstone.

COOMEY M. and STEPHENSON J. (2001)

'Online learning: it is all about dialogue, involvement, support and control – according to research'. In J. Stephenson (ed.) *Teaching and Learning Online*. London, Kogan Page.

CROWDER M. and PUPYNIN K. (1993)

The Motivation to Train. Research Series No. 9. Sheffield, The Employment Dept.

DAVENPORT T.H. (2001)

eLearning and the Attention Economy: Here, there and everywhere? Learning in the New Economy, Spring 2001 – at: www.linezine.com/5.2/articles/tdeatae.htm

DAVIS S. and MEYER C. (1998)

BLUR: The speed of change in the connected economy. Oxford, Capstone.

DENNISON W. F. and KIRK R. (1990)

Do, Review, Learn, Apply: A simple guide to experimental learning. Oxford, Blackwell.

DEWEY J. (1969)

Experience and Education. London, Collier-Macmillan.

DOBBS K. (2000)

'Simple moments of learning'. *Training*. Vol. 37, No.1. pp52–4.

DREYFUS H. L. and DREYFUS S. E. (1986)

Mind over Machine: The power of human intuition and expertise in the era of the computer. Oxford, Basil Blackwell.

ENGESTROM Y. and MIDDLETON D. (eds) (1996)

Cognition and Communication at Work. Cambridge, Cambridge University Press.

ERAUT M. (1994)

Developing Professional Knowledge and Competence. London, Falmer Press.

FELDER R. (1996)

'Matters of style'. *ASEE Prism*. Vol. 6, No. 4. pp18–23, December – at: www2.ncsu.edu/unity/lockers/users/f/felder/public/Papers/LS-Prism.htm

FESTINGER L. (1957)

A Theory of Cognitive Dissonance. Evanston, Ill., Row, Peterson and Company.

FISCHER G. and SCHARFF E. (1998)

'Learning technologies in support of self-directed learning'. *Journal of Interactive Media in Education*. Vol. 98, No. 4 – at: www-jime.open.ac.uk/98/4

GAGNÉ R. M. (1966)

The Conditions of Learning. New York, Holt, Rinehart and Winston.

GARDNER H. (1983)

Frames of Mind: The theory of multiple intelligences. New York, Basic Books – see also: www.pz.harvard.edu/WhatsNew/Amsterdam.htm

GORAWARA-BHAT R. (2000)

The Social and Spatial Ecology of Work: The case of a survey research organization. New York, Kluwer Academic/Plenum Publishers.

HANDY C. (1985)

Understanding Organisations. London, Penguin.

HARASIM L., HILTZ S., TELES L. and TUROFF M. (1995)

Learning Networks. Cambridge, Mass., MIT Press.

HERZBERG F. (1968)

Work and the Nature of Man. London, Staples Press.

HERZBERG F., MAUSNER B. and SNYDERMAN B. (1959)

The Motivation to Work. New York, John Wiley & Sons.

HILL W. F. (1990)

Learning: A survey of psychological interpretations. 5th edition. New York, Harper & Row.

HOWARD K. W. (1989)

'A comprehensive expectancy motivation model: implications for adult education and training'. *Adult Education Quarterly*. Vol. 39, No. 4. pp199–210.

ICAEW (2001)

Human Capital: From cutting edge to mainstream practice? Key points from a Centre for Business Performance roundtable. Briefing 05.01, Centre for Business Performance, The Institute of Chartered Accountants in England & Wales, May.

IET (2000)

Virtual Degree Ceremony. Institute of Educational Technology, The Open University – at: kmi.open.ac.uk/projects/vdc

JENNINGS C. (1999)

Where Does Online Learning End and Knowledge Management Begin? Online Educa Berlin, 5th International Conference on Technology Supported Learning, November.

KEEGAN D. (1996)

Foundations of Distance Education. London, Routledge.

KNOWLEDGENET (2001)

Exploding the e-Learning Myth: Next-generation, web-based training is here today – and it delivers the 'wow' experience. White Paper, KnowledgeNet.com – at: www.knowledgenet.com/newsroom/whitepapers/elearningmyth.jsp

KNOWLES M. S. (1980)

Modern Practice of Adult Education: From pedagogy to androgogy. 2nd edition. Chicago, Association Press.

KOLB D. A. (1984)

Experiential Learning: Experience as the source of learning and development. Englewood Cliffs, NJ, Prentice-Hall.

KOSCHMANN T. (ed.) (1996)

CSCL: Theory and practice. Hillsdale, NJ, Erlbaum.

LAM A. (2000)

'Tacit knowledge, organization studies and societal institutions: an integrated framework'. *Organizational Studies.* Vol. 21, No. 3. pp487–513.

LANDAUER R. (1995)

The Trouble with Computers. Cambridge, Mass., MIT Press.

LAURILLARD D. (1993)

Rethinking University Teaching: A framework for the effective use of educational technology. London, Routledge.

LAVE J. and WENGER E. (1991)

Situated Learning: Legitimate peripheral participation. Cambridge, Cambridge University Press.

LEADBEATER C. (2001)

'Learning and work – authorship'. In CIPD *The Future of Learning for Work.* London, Chartered Institute of Personnel and Development, p33.

LIM C. P. (2001)

What Isn't E-Learning. TechKnowLogia, May/June, Knowledge Enterprise – at: www.techknowlogia.org/TKL_active_pages2/CurrentArticles/main.asp?FileType=PDF&ArticleID=267

LOCKE E. A., SHAW K. N., SAARI L. M. and LATHAM G. P. (1981)

'Goal-setting and task performance: 1969–1980'. *Psychological Bulletin.* Vol. 90, No. 1. pp125–52.

MARTIN G., PATE J. and BEAUMONT P. (2001)

'Company-based education programmes: what's the pay-off for employers?' *Human Resources Management Journal.* Vol. 11, No. 4. pp55–73.

MASIE E. (2000)

'Learning at our busy desks?' *Learning Decisions.* May.

MASLOW A. H. (1968)

Toward a Psychology of Being. New York, Van Nostrand Reinhold.

MASLOW A. H. (1987)

Motivation and Personality. 3rd edition. New York, Harper & Row.

MASON R. (1991)

Moderating Educational Computer Conferencing. emoderators.com, Vol. 1, No. 19 – at: www.emoderators.com/papers/mason.html

MASON R. (1999)

IET's Masters in Open and Distance Education: What have we learned? – at: icdl.open.ac.uk/lit2k/LitResult.ihtml?&id=16562

MASON R. and WELLER M. (2000)

'Factors affecting students' satisfaction on a Web course'. *Australian Journal of Educational Technology.* Vol. 16, No. 2. pp173–200 – at: cleo.murdoch.edu.au/ajet/ajet16/mason.html

MEZIROW J. (1983)

'A critical theory of adult learning and education'. In M. Tight (ed.) *Education for Adults: Volume 1: Adult learning and education.* London, Croom Helm.

NIPPER S. (1989)

'Third-generation distance learning and computer conferencing'. In R. Mason and A. Kaye (eds) *Mindweave: Communication, computers and distance education.* Oxford, Pergamon Press.

NONAKA I. AND TAKEUCHI H. (1995)

The Knowledge Creating Company: How Japanese companies create the dynamics of innovation. Oxford, Oxford University Press.

O'CONNOR T. (1997)

Using Learning Styles to Adapt Technology for Higher Education. Center for Teaching and Learning, Indiana State University – also at: web.indstate.edu/ctl/styles/learning.html

PIAGET J. (1950)

The Psychology of Intelligence. London, Routledge & Kegan Paul.

PIAGET J. (1963)

'The attainment of invariants and reversible operations in the development of thinking'. *Social Research.* Vol. 30. pp283–99 (presented at the University of Chicago on 3 April 1953).

QUINN A. (2001)

Why People can't Use eLearning. Frontend.com, June – at: infocentre.frontend.com/servlet/Infocentre

ROGERS A. (1996)

Teaching Adults. 2nd edition. London, Open University Press.

ROGERS C. R. (1961)

On Becoming a Person: A therapist's view of psychotherapy. London, Constable & Company (latest edition: Houghton Mifflin, Boston, 1995).

ROGERS C. R. (1983)

Freedom to Learn. 2nd edition. Columbus, Ohio, Charles E. Merrill Publishing Company.

ROY D. (1959)

'Banana time: job satisfaction and informal interaction'. *Human Organisation.* Vol. 18. pp158–68.

RYLE G. (1949)

The Concept of Mind. Harmondsworth, Peregrine Books.

SAVIN-BADEN M. (2001)

'(Dis)placed academics? Staff experiences of role change in the context of problem-based learning'. Presented at BERA 2001, University of Leeds, 14–15 September.

SCARBOROUGH H., SWAN J. AND PRESTON J. (1999)

Knowledge Management: A literature review. London, Institute of Personnel and Development.

SCHANK R. C. (1997)

Virtual Learning: A revolutionary way to build a highly skilled workforce. New York, McGraw Hill.

SCHEIN E. H. (1980)

Organisational Psychology. New Jersey, Prentice-Hall.

SCHÖN D. A. (1983)

The Reflective Practitioner: How professionals think in action. New York, Basic Books.

SCHREIBER D. (1998)

'Best practices of distance training'. In D. Schreiber *and* Z. Berge (eds) *Distance Training.* San Francisco, Jossey-Bass.

SCHULTZ T. W. (1961)

'Investment in human capital'. *The American Economic Review.* Vol. 51, No. 1. pp1–17.

SENGE P. M. (1990)

The Fifth Discipline: The art and practice of the learning organization. New York, Doubleday.

SKINNER B. F. (1974)

About Behaviourism. London, Jonathan Cape.

SKINNER B. F. (2001)

A Brief Survey of Operant Behavior. B.F. Skinner Foundation – at: www.bfskinner.org/operant.asp

SLOMAN M. (2001)

The E-Learning Revolution. London, Chartered Institute of Personnel and Development.

SMITH M. K. (1997)

Carl Rogers, Core Conditions and Education. infed.org – at: http://www.infed.org/thinkers/et-rogers.htm

SPECTOR J. and ANDERSON R. (eds) (2000)

Integrated and Holistic Perspectives on Learning and Instruction: Understanding complexity. Dordrecht, Kluwer.

SPECTOR M. (2001)

'Foreword'. In C. Steeples and C. Jones (eds) *Computer Supported Cooperative Work.* London, Springer.

STAMPS D. (1998)

'Learning ecologies'. *Training.* Vol. 35, No. 1. pp32–8.

STEPHENSON J. (2001)

'Learner-managed learning – an emerging pedagogy for learning online'. In J. Stephenson (ed.) *Teaching and Learning Online.* London, Kogan Page.

STERN E. and SOMMERLAD E. (1999)

Workplace Learning, Culture and Performance. London, Institute of Personnel and Development.

TELEEDUCATION NEW BRUNSWICK (2001)

The 'No Significant Difference' Phenomenon. TeleEducation New Brunswick – at: teleeducation.nb.ca/nosignificantdifference/

TENNANT M. (1997)

Psychology and Adult Learning. 2nd edition. London, Routledge.

TIGHT M. (1996)

Key Concepts in Adult Education and Training. London, Routledge.

THORNDIKE E. L. (1911)

Animal Intelligence. New York, The Macmillan Company.

TORRANCE E. P. and ROCKENSTEIN Z. L. (1988)

'Styles of thinking and creativity'. In R. R. Schmeck (ed.) *Learning Strategies and Learning Styles.* New York, Plenum Press.

URDAN R. and WEGGEN C. (2001)

E-Learning: Outlook for the learning management system market. W.R.Hambrecht and Co. – at: www.wrhambrecht.com/research/elearning/ir/index.html

VROOM V. H. (1964)

Work and Motivation. New York, John Wiley & Sons (reprinted in 1994 by Jossey-Bass, San Franciso).

VYGOTSKY L. S. (1962)

Thought and Language. Cambridge, Mass., MIT Press.

VYGOTSKY L. S. (1978)

Mind in Society: The development of higher psychological processes. Cambridge, Mass., Harvard University Press.

WAGNER R. G. AND STERNBERG R. J. (1986)

'Tacit knowledge and intelligence in the everyday world'. In R. J. Sternberg and R. G. Wagner (eds) *Practical Intelligence: Nature and origins of competence in the everyday world.* Cambridge, Cambridge University Press.

WEINER B. (1990)

'History of motivational research in education'. *Journal of Educational Psychology.* Vol. 82, No. 4. pp616–22.

WENGER E. (1998)

Communities of Practice: Learning, meaning and identity. Cambridge, Cambridge University Press.